D1343299

rlotta Schiroli

Women's Football: Motivations and Future Perspectives

Carlotta Schiroli

Women's Football: Motivations and Future Perspectives

An insight about motivations of Women's Football
players and a future perspective towards the
development of this sport

Social Sciences Series

Impressum / Imprint

Bibliografische Information der Deutschen Nationalbibliothek: Die Deutsche Nationalbibliothek verzeichnet diese Publikation in der Deutschen Nationalbibliografie; detaillierte bibliografische Daten sind im Internet über http://dnb.d-nb.de abrufbar.
Alle in diesem Buch genannten Marken und Produktnamen unterliegen warenzeichen-, marken- oder patentrechtlichem Schutz bzw. sind Warenzeichen oder eingetragene Warenzeichen der jeweiligen Inhaber. Die Wiedergabe von Marken, Produktnamen, Gebrauchsnamen, Handelsnamen, Warenbezeichnungen u.s.w. in diesem Werk berechtigt auch ohne besondere Kennzeichnung nicht zu der Annahme, dass solche Namen im Sinne der Warenzeichen- und Markenschutzgesetzgebung als frei zu betrachten wären und daher von jedermann benutzt werden dürften.

Bibliographic information published by the Deutsche Nationalbibliothek: The Deutsche Nationalbibliothek lists this publication in the Deutsche Nationalbibliografie; detailed bibliographic data are available in the Internet at http://dnb.d-nb.de.
Any brand names and product names mentioned in this book are subject to trademark, brand or patent protection and are trademarks or registered trademarks of their respective holders. The use of brand names, product names, common names, trade names, product descriptions etc. even without a particular marking in this works is in no way to be construed to mean that such names may be regarded as unrestricted in respect of trademark and brand protection legislation and could thus be used by anyone.

Coverbild / Cover image: www.ingimage.com

Verlag / Publisher:
AV Akademikerverlag
ist ein Imprint der / is a trademark of
OmniScriptum GmbH & Co. KG
Heinrich-Böcking-Str. 6-8, 66121 Saarbrücken, Deutschland / Germany
Email: info@akademikerverlag.de

Herstellung: siehe letzte Seite /
Printed at: see last page
ISBN: 978-3-639-49993-3

Abstract

Motivation is at the heart of many sports' most interesting issues. The level of motivation of an athlete can make the difference between obtaining or losing the pre-established performance's objectives and this is a crucial concept in the sport's world. What comes immediately to our mind is: Why do people practise sport? What are the main motivations? My research wants to investigate the main motivations that initially pushed and are currently pushing female athletes to practise football. As everybody knows Women's football is a minor sport. My work wants aims to investigate the difficulties and the lacks of women's football, trying to understand where to start in order to develop this sport. In order to develop my research I took into consideration two important motivation theories, *Self Determinant Theory* (SDT) and *Achievement Goal Theory* (AGT) and I based the creation of the questionnaire on the *Sport Motivation Scale* (SMS). My analysis has been done through the collection of quantitative data with the help of questionnaires and qualitative data with an interview to a person directly involved in the women's football world. The results of my investigation show that women are initially extrinsic motivated toward the practise of football while are currently pushed by the Intrinsic Motivation to experience stimulation with both influence of *Task* and *Ego orientation*. Concerning women's football, athletes consider media attention and sponsors as the main factors that could help women's football in its development. Moreover athletes expect from the FIFA Women World Cup an increment of media attention and sponsors for women's football.

Abstract

Die Motivation steht im Zentrum vieler interessanter Fragen des Sports. Das Motivationsniveau einer Athletin kann den Unterschied zwischen Erhalt und Verlust der vorgegebenen Performance-Ziele ausmachen, und dies ist einer der entscheidenden Punkte in der Welt des Sports. Und was einem sofort dazu einfällt ist: Warum treiben die Menschen Sport? Welches sind die Hauptgründe dafür?. Mit meiner Diplomarbeit möchte ich untersuchen, welches die Beweggründe sind, die die Athletinnen anfangs und auch derzeit dazu bewegen, Fussball als Sportart zu praktizieren. Wie jeder weiß, nimmt der Frauenfussball nur eine untergeordnete Rolle in der Welt des Sports ein. Mit meiner Recherche möchte ich herausfinden, welchen Schwierigkeiten und Unterschieden der Frauenfussball sich heutzutage zu stellen hat, um zu verstehen, welches die fundamentalen Ausgangspunkte sind, diese Sportart weiterzuentwickeln. Bei meiner Arbeit sind mir zwei wichtige Motivationstheorien behilflich gewesen, und zwar die *Self Determinant Theory* (SDT) und die *Achievement Goal Theory* (AGT). Darüber hinaus habe ich mich bei der Erstellung meines Fragebogens auf die *Sport Motivation Scale* (SMS) gestützt, eine Skala, die die verschiedenen Motivationsarten klassifiziert, die die Athleten zur Ausübung einer bestimmten Sportart bringt. Die Analyse kam zustande durch das Zusammentragen von quantitativen Daten mit Hilfe der Fragebögen und der qualitativen Daten durch ein Interview mit einer Person, die direkt in die Welt des Frauenfussballs involviert ist. Die Resultate meiner Untersuchungen haben ergeben, dass weibliche Personen sich auf der einen Seite bei der Ausübung des Fussballsports von äusseren Motivationen (*Extrinsic Motivation*) beeinflussen lassen aber heutzutage auch durch eigene (*Intrinsic Motivation*) Motivation; sie sind sowohl aufgabenorientiert (*task oriented*) als auch ego-orientiert (*ego oriented*). Was den Frauenfussball betrifft, denken die Athletinnen, dass die Aufmerksamkeit der Medien und der Sponsoren die wichtigsten Faktoren sind, den Frauenfussball weiterzuentwickeln. Darüber hinaus erwarten die Athletinnen, dass die Frauenfussball-WM genau das bringen wird, was ihnen bis jetzt fehlt, d.h. Aufmerksamkeit von Seiten der Medien und der Sponsoren.

Abstract

La motivazione sta al centro di molte ed interessanti questioni riguardo lo sport. Il livello di motivazione di un atleta può fare la differenza tra ottenere o mancare gli obiettivi di performance prestabiliti e questo è un punto cruciale nel mondo dello sport. Ciò che viene subito da pensare è: Perchè le persone praticano sport? Quali sono le maggiori motivazioni? La mia tesi vuole esaminare quali sono le motivazioni che inizialmente hanno spinto e che correntemente spingono le atlete nella pratica del calcio. Come è noto a tutti, il calcio femminile è uno sport minore. Con la mia ricerca voglio andare a verificare quali sono le difficoltà e le lacune che si trova ad affrontare il calcio femminile odierno, cercando di capire quali sono i punti fondamentali dai quali partire per sviluppare questo sport. In questo mio scopo mi sono state d'aiuto due importanti teorie sulla motivazione, la *Self Determinant Theory* (SDT) e la *Achievement Goal Theory* (AGT). Inoltre per la creazione del questionario mi sono basata sulla *Sport Motivation Scale* (SMS), una scala che classifica vari tipi di motivazioni che spingono gli atleti verso la pratica di un determinato sport. L'analisi è stata fatta grazie alla raccolta di dati quantitativi tramite la somministrazione di un questionario e di dati qualitativi con un'intervista ad una persona direttamente coinvolta nel mondo del calcio femminile. I risultati della mia ricerca hanno evidenziato che le ragazze sono inizialmente influenzate da motivazioni estrinseche verso la pratica del calcio, mentre sono attualmente spinte da motivazioni intrinseche e risultano essere anche *task oriented* ed *ego oriented*. Per quanto riguarda il calcio femminile, le atlete pensano che l'attenzione da parte dei media e gli sponsor, siano i fattori di maggiore importanza che potrebbero aiutare lo sviluppo del calcio femminile. Inoltre le atlete si aspettano che i Campionati Mondiali di calcio femminile portino esattamente cioè che ad esso manca e cioè sponsor e attenzione da parte dei media.

Table of contents

Chapter 1

Introduction

The world of sports is continuously growing and with it also the environment that surrounds this world has grown the attention to sports. Mass Media focused their attention on sports dedicating more time to sport channels, sport pages in newspapers and entire magazines. There is a consistent part of the population that define themselves as interested in following sports even if only a small minority of the population are actually active participants. Sports are nowadays implicated with education, internationalism, globalization and mass media. Sport is everywhere. It helps individuals to better know themselves, to acknowledge their limits, to get in touch with their own physical and to socialize. Sport is something that can come naturally as a gift that we must develop and implement or something that can be instilled and taught. It combines talent, passion, effort, strategic thinking, and physical predominance with rules, respect, devotion, friendship and loyalty. Naturally we cannot forget that sport is in someway associated with conflicts, racism, sexual discriminations and other problems that afflicts the new conception of sport. What I really think is that these disappointing aspects that unfortunately are found not only in our society, but also in the Sport's world are becoming anachronistic and non-sensing. If we take a look at our growing and changing society we would notice that lot has been done to help the integration, to fight against gender discrimination, sexual orientation and racism but still lot has to be done. These problems must be overcome because nobody can own sport, nobody can be excluded or can be taken apart; as I said before, Sport is found everywhere, also in boundary situations where the ball is made of papers and an athlete could be potentially found in everyone. Sport is beautiful and everyone could be the possibility to get in touch with this world regardless of skin colour, sexual orientation, religion, political orientation and gender.

Although sport has gained much more respect and interest from experts and studies, some still express surprise that the subject is considered appropriate for academic analysis. Some people view sport as a world that lies apart from the rest of society. Actually, what can be very interesting and attractive is exactly this apartness. The fact that sport can be considered something apart from everything else may represent his appeal from the participants and spectators point of view. Indeed, Sport is something unique and his world hides and endless number of incredible surprises.

For this reason when I had to choose my thesis' topic, I decided to take into consideration different aspects of sport.

In this thesis, the literature review begins with a chapter about the Sport motivation and the theories that has been developed about this topic. These two theories are called SDT (Self Determinant Theory) and AGT (Achievement Goal Theory). In this chapter I also examined the SMS (Sport Motivation Scale) that it was useful to me for the creation of my questionnaire. Moreover I found another interesting aspect related to sport motivation that are coaches, peers and parents influence on athletes motivation.

The following chapter is about women's sport. This is because this research focuses mainly on women's football. I wanted to analyse some specific aspects of women's sport so I decided to write about the inequalities between genders. It is actually a real interesting aspect that requires more than one paragraph or chapter and maybe an entire thesis about this topic would result not sufficient to explain everything about it. Although I could spend not too much words about that, I wanted however to try to give a general overview about this topic.

Further I faced another aspect of gender inequalities in sport; it is the relationship between sport and mass media attention. More in specific I analyzed the differences of mass media attention between women's sport and male's sport. In order to link this chapter with the previous one and the successive I added an interesting paragraph about women's motivation toward sport. It is a short paragraph, but it helped me to have a general overview about this specific issue.

The literature review continues with women's football. In particular I examined the situation in Italy starting from the birth of Italian's women football. Due to the important women's football development I chose to analyze also the situation in USA. Than, I wrote about the aspect of women's football and mass media, that is still an interesting topic.

My thesis deals with the motivations and the future perspectives of women's football. I decided to face these topics principally because I am a passionate player and fun of football. Than, I found interesting to try to deepen a topic such as motivation toward the practise of sport that actually lays apart from all the general treated topics. The question I asked my self was: Why do people practise sport? Why women's football players decide everyday to practise this sport despite all the problems and the difficulties that come out?

As I know the problems that women's football must face everyday to survive I wanted also to try to give an overview about the major problems and difficulties of this sport. However my intention was not only to find and list the lacks and problems of women's football but I also tried to give some possible solutions to these problems. Thanks to the questionnaire I created, I was able to investigate and understand the athletes' point of view about different topics.

The main aim of my thesis is to find out what are the factors that initially and currently push women players in the practise of football. To help my investigation I used the two motivation theories (AGT and SDT) and the sport motivation scale (SMS). Thanks to these I am able to understand the type and the efficacy of the main motivations.

Another objective of my thesis is to understand what are the lacks and what could be the crucial points for the development of women's football from the athlete's point of view.

Finally with my research I wanted to define specific characteristics of different groups of women football players.

The rest of the present work is divided in three sections.

The first one is the literature review divided in three chapters: sport motivation, women's sport and women's football.

The second section presents the research objectives and the methodology used to collect and analyse the data.

The third section outlines the results of the primary research, the interview with Mr. Roberto Genta (journalist specialised in women's football) and provides a discussion of the findings.

Chapter 2

Sport Motivation and Theories

The study of motivation is not simple and faces lot of difficulties. First problem is to find out an appropriate definition of motivation. For example, De Beni and Moè (2000), give this definition of motivation: "something that explain us the beginning, the direction, the intensity and the persistence of a behaviour toward an aim." Other authors as Hagger and Chatzisarantis define motivation as "an internal state that activates, energizes, or drives action or behaviour". Many other authors gave their own and personal definition of motivation and all of them are right. Another difficulty is that the same behaviour can reflect different motivations and the same motivation can lead to different behaviours. Actually the real problem is that a person is not necessarily aware of the "why" of his/her actions.

2.1 SPORT MOTIVATION

Motivation is at the heart of many sports' most interesting issues. The level of motivation of an athlete can make the difference between obtaining or losing the pre-established performance's objectives and this is a crucial concept in the sport's world. What comes immediately to our mind is: Why do people practise sport? What are the main motivations?

The dream of every coach would be to have self-motivated athletes that train themselves always with the maximal concentration and with high engagement. Of course we know that it is still impossible to find such a perfect athlete and we know also that sport motivation can be influenced from many different factors.

During the last years, people showed an increasing interest about the sport motivational topic and for this reason many researches and studies were conducted.

Vanek and Cratty (1972) created a really interesting outline about the primary, secondary and social motivations that push individuals toward the practise of sport. They did some studies during which more than 600 athletes were studied. The most general motivations were "the need to perform physical activity" and "the need for success". They took as assumption that these two motivations exist in every human being, even if in different levels. Obviously every individual has different grade of feeling the need to practise sport that is related to his/her age, lifestyle and the environment. In addiction to these two types three more motivations come: "the need for novelty", "the need for stability" and "the need to predict situations" that he/she will face. However the authors also state that it is extremely difficult to find out the specific motivations present in an athlete because there are too many variables to take into consideration. Another consideration that we can make is that individuals are surrounded by lot of variables that can influence them in every moment: it can be the political, social or economical situation. Exactly at support of this statement Cratty (1974) conducted a study about the nature of the human motivations and he examined also the social motivations that sometimes can be more important than the needs related to the physiological sphere. The success or the failure of a sport performance can make the athlete gaining or losing some social level; also for young people the success in a sport competition can be very useful to gain social importance.

Another author, Bouet (1974), wrote about the psychological secrets of sport and he conducted a research about the sport motivations. He gave 1.634 questionnaires to athletes of both genders of different ages, socio-economical environment and different sports disciplines and levels of qualification. After analysing some basic motivations and sport motivations as "the need for movement", he focused on the need for self-determination.

Self-determination is related to the possibility to better understand some parts of our personality. All individuals have the need to know their own limits and the need to understand their own possibilities. Sport becomes a way through which persons can get in touch with some traits of their personality that otherwise could never be discovered. I will discuss more about the self-determination in the next sub-chapter.

2.1.1 Self Determinant Theory

Different research studies about self-determination were conducted, but in particular two authors, Deci and Ryan, developed a theory based on self-determination, also called self-determinant theory (SDT). This research provides a comprehensive understanding of motivational processes; more precisely it states that different types of motivation represent the tendency to differentiate, integrate and actualize oneself within his/her environment. In other words SDT helps to investigate the tendencies of people's personal growth and innate psychological needs that are the basis for their self-motivation and personality integration (Deci & Ryan, 2000). Moreover Deci & Ryan (2000) and Vansteenkiste (2005), they state that SDT also pays attention to the type of goals that people pursue through behaviour. So we can distinguish between two types of goals or motivations; the first are intrinsic goals or intrinsic motivations (IM) (i.e affiliation, self-development, health and physical fitness), which are directly related to the tendency of individuals to a personal growth. As Ryan (1995) says, these intrinsic goals tend to be associated with the needs for autonomy, competence and relatedness. The other type of goals are called extrinsic goals or extrinsic motivations (EM) (i.e power, physical attractiveness and financial success), which are related to the tendency of people to impress others by acquiring external signs of worth, it means that there is an external push that moves people's actions that can come for example from peers, coaches and also parents. It refers to doing an activity for external outcomes.

Some studies confirm that people with higher levels of self-determined motivation can do better performances, can manage in better way stressful situations and invest more effort in activities. Vallerand (1997) supports Deci and Ryan (1985) saying that motivation is multidimensional and argued that the varying types of motivation could explain much of human behaviour and therefore must be included in a comprehensive analysis of motivation.

2.1.2 Sport Motivation Scale

Among the self-determinant theory, a sport-context motivation measure, the Sport Motivation Scale (SMS), has been developed. After some researches, this theoretical approach is finally considered to be pertinent to the field of sport. In line with SDT, the aim of the SMS, is to measure what kind of forces push the individuals to practise sport under different points of view.

The Sport Motivation Scale (SMS) consists of seven subscales that measure three types of Intrinsic Motivation (IM to Know, IM to Accomplish Things, and IM to Experience Stimulation), three forms of regulation for Extrinsic Motivation (Identified, Introjected, and External), and Amotivation. (Pelletier, Tuson, Brière, Fortier, Vallerand, 1995). But let me clarify these different types of Motivation.

2.1.2.1   Intrinsic Motivation

Intrinsic motivation refers to engaging in an activity purely for the pleasure and satisfaction derived from doing the activity (Deci, 1975). As we can find in an academic article by Pelletier, Tuson, Brière, Fortier, Vallerand (1995), athletes intrinsically motivated toward sport, find interesting and satisfying to learn more about this discipline or they practise sport for the pleasure of constantly trying to surpass themselves. Moreover, all the activities that make the individuals experience a feeling of competence and self-determination are said to dealing with IM. For this reason, Deci and Ryan (2000) state that IM comes from the innate psychological needs for competence and self-determination. We can distinguish between three types of IM that have been identified: IM to Know, IM to Accomplish Things, and IM to Experience Stimulation.

- *Instrinsic Motivation to Know*

Following the definition of Pelletier, Tuson, Brière, Fortier, Vallerand, (1995), we can say that IM to know can be defined as performing an activity for the pleasure and the satisfaction that a person experiences while learning, exploring, or trying to understand something new. An example of *IM to Know* can be an athlete that experiences pleasure and satisfaction while trying to discover new training techniques. This motivation type is strictly related with learning goals, curiosity and exploration.

- *Intrinsic Motivation Toward Accomplishments*

This type of IM is referred to those activities that are done for the merely pleasure and in order to experience satisfaction. Persons behave in this way to feel competent and to create unique accomplishment. For example, an athlete intrinsically motivated toward accomplishment, experiences personal satisfaction trying to master some difficult training techniques.

- *Intrinsic Motivation to Experience Stimulation*

It occurs when athletes that participate in a specific sport activity, do it in order to live exciting experiences. A person is said to be intrinsically motivated when he/she performs an activity in order to experiencing stimulating experiences.

2.1.2.2   Extrinsic Motivation

If we speak about extrinsic motivation we relate it to a large variety of behaviours, which are engaged not for their own benefit but rather as a means to an end. In origin it was thought that extrinsic motivation was related to non-self-determined behaviour but recent studies have stated that actually there are different types of extrinsic motivation that can be located along a self-determinant continuum. They are: external regulation, introjection, and identification.

- *External Regulation*

It refers to every behaviour that is imposed and controlled by the externals as constraints that are imposed by others, or material rewards. An example can be an athlete that is motivated by his coach in order to receive money or the motivation can start from the pushes of the parents. In these occasions sport is performed to avoid negative consequences and not for just experience fun.

- *Introjection*

In the Introjection there is the presence of external push and motivations as described for external regulation, but also the behaviours are influenced by the athlete himself that feels internal pressure as guilt or anxiety. For example athletes who are under pressure because they must feel in a good shape for aesthetic reasons, otherwise they are not they feel ashamed.

- *Identification*

Identified motivations relate to athletes that decide to do sport because they feel that in this way they can grow and develop as a person. These individuals value and judge actions as important and necessary for they own growth and they perform it out of choice.

- *Amotivation*

This is the final form of motivation that is quite different from the others. Persons who feel amotivated are those who are neither intrinsically nor extrinsically motivated.

So speaking about the sport's field we can state that the three types of IM and Identification can be associated with positive emotions, greater interest and sport satisfaction. Moreover, according to Brière et al. (2010), we can declare that the more athletes see themselves as competent and self-determined, the more they appear self-determined and motivated toward sport.

2.1.3 Achievement Goal Theory

The Achievement Goal Theory (AGT) is considered to be very interesting in relation with motivation. Before we start discussing AGT we must say that many goals and goal orientation models were studied during the years (Nicholls, 1984;

Elliot, 1997; Dweck & Leggett, 1988) and these models vary in the number of goals, the approaches to the goals and also in the definition of what goal is. I decided to focus on this interesting theory because, in my opinion, it can perfectly be adjusted to the Sport's world.

Although achievement's factors are many and various, we must state that one of the primary elements of achievement is motivation (Maehr and Zusho, 2009). It is also interesting to explore this theory under a sport's point of view. We can start saying that individuals focus on demonstrating competence in achievement situations and these achievement goals may be related to how individuals view themselves in certain situations. As we can find in an article by Pintrich, Conley, Kempler (2003), "Achievement goal orientations represent the individual's 'orientation' to the task or situation, their general focus or purpose for achievement, and not just the specific target goal they have for the task".

As Hagger and Chatzisarantis (2005) write, we can distinguish between two different motivational tendencies that prevail in achievement situations: a *task orientation* and an *ego orientation*. When an athlete is task orientated, he would like to get in touch with himself, he is pleased when he can learn new skills and when he can improve himself. For example a rugby player may view success in the number of goals and passes he completed relative to the past match or season. While if we consider an athlete that is ego-oriented, he would like to demonstrate his competence basically competing with the others and he will see his success in beating the opponent or in being in a higher rank compared to others. He will be indifferent to the possibility to improve himself while he will be motivated by the desire to improve his ego. What we have to take into consideration is that although these two orientations are independent from each other it could be possible to find an individual that has high level of both at the same time.

If we go further, we can observe that this Achievement Goal Theory becomes very interesting and useful for motivation predictions if we consider it in the failure situations. It means that in case of failure, as for example the defeat, an athlete with low task orientation but high ego orientation will experience a strong decrease in the level of motivation related to managing the same behaviour again. While taking into consideration an athlete in the same situation but that is highly task oriented (or task oriented only, with low ego orientation), he will experience success related with the achievement of personal goals regardless of failure.

For this reason we are led to believe that the task orientation are signals of an internal motivation that can be associated with satisfaction and persistence. This type of motivation is called intrinsic motivation as we saw before with the SDT. A person with high-task orientation tends to see the success in a determined situation for internal reasons regardless of objective outcomes. Thus, achievement goal theory motivational constructs from self-determinant theory.

2.1.4 Coaches, Peers and Parents influence in Sport Motivation

There is increasing evidence that peers and parents in the sporting context, as well as coaches, all play important roles in influencing motivation.

About this topic many researches were conducted, in particular I want to focus on one study found on an article by Keegan, Harwood, Spray, Lavallee (2009). It examines the motivational influences of coaches, parents and peers in the early career of sport participants.

As written in this article "when studying the social influences on motivation of young athletes participating in sport, one is examining the reasons behind motivated actions and the ways in which coaches, parents and peers can influence these reasons. These three social agents, taken together, may be influential across the vast majority of the athlete's sporting experience".

From this study appears that coaches and parents have a relatively strong influence on athlete motivation, maybe due to their singular positions of authority, while peer influences tend to be different to coaches and parents and it appears to at this specific stage less significant.

Focusing on coach influence on sport's motivation, we can find also lot of research studies that support the credence that coaches' behaviours are relevant determinants of athletes' motivation.

Therefore, I found interesting another article by Gillet, Vallerand, Amoura , Baldes (2010), where the authors conducted a study about the perceptions of coach behaviours, motivation, and sport performance in order to better understand the determinants of athletes' performance.

The result of the study was that, the more the athletes perceived their coach to be autonomy-supportive, the more their motivation for practicing their sport activity was self-determined.

Chapter 3

Women's Sport

3.1 INEQUALITIES BETWEEN GENDERS

Women had always faced lot of difficulties to enter the world of politics and of culture, but actually they had more problems to enter the sport's world.

Nowadays, Sport is considered to be a well-developed phenomenon in both genders. Although the strong evolution of women's sport during the last decades, story tells us that the male gender had always had the predominance in the practise of sport. Actually some forms of inequalities are still present; for example male's sport is considered to be more relevant both economically and culturally speaking. (Sassatelli, 2003)

Since the middle-class society is typically male, it appears obvious that the modern sport fit perfectly with men. On the contrary, the practise of physical activity for women was considered to be unethical. Also De Coubertin, the inventor of the Olympic Games, was contrary to the women's sport.

The major differences between genders related to the sport's field are based on the natural traits of male and women. Sport had always given to the men the possibility to highlight and show their masculine characters and to implement their virile image, relegating the women to be the passive and subdued part. So women were seen as passive and weak. The diffused credence saw the women athletes as deviated from their natural pure image and as not normal and absolutely to be stopped. Some sports, as for example boxe or rugby, are seen as being suitable only for male because of the need of a body particularly strong, big and muscled. Very interesting is what feminists thought about this problem. They tended to see the differences and inequalities between women and men in the sport's world as a social construction. As Nixon and Howard (2008) write,

"Because we are born with certain biological or sex differences as male and female, people have often assumed that differences in gender identities and roles traditionally associated with sex differences, are natural."

So it appears clear that the major obstacle for the development of women's sport was the diffused social prejudice. With these thoughts women's sport faced difficulties to emerge also because women athletes were considered to losing their femininity while performing some physical activities.

The most common error is to consider the male and feminine as a principle of symmetry, so woman as opposite of man and vice-versa. According to the sport's world this is not true and this consideration makes women athletes losing their possibility to be seen as normal woman and also as merely engaged athletes.

Fortunately thanks to the women's emancipation and with the conquer of some equalities between gender, sport is not more seen as deviating or unsuitable for women. The conquer of a place in the sport's world was slow and difficult and it was also stopped by the general declarations from many scientists that said how inappropriate was sport for women.

Today female athletes can use sport as a way to demonstrate and show their personality. This does not mean that all the prejudices are suddenly disappeared. Some studies demonstrated that women, who devoted their life to sports, and particularly to football, are more self-determinate, ambitious and intentioned to reach the pre-established objectives than the male colleagues.

3.2 MASS MEDIA AND MINOR/NICHE SPORTS

Sport appears to be the perfectly suitable tool for mass media not only because it provides a big space availability but also because it matches the show of the game with the unpredictability of the results. If we take a look on which sports gain most of the attention from the mass media, there are large differences.

Obviously, sports with many followers and athletes receive big space and attention from the mass media, as for example football in Italy and basket, hockey and baseball in the US. On one side of the medal, popular sports receive large national and international media coverage with lot of daily news broadcasted on television and present on the newspapers. On the other side of the medal there are those sports that for many different reasons face lot of difficulties to emerge. We can call these types of sports as minor sports or niche sports.

Actually the definition of minor or niche sport can bring to a wrong conclusion; it is not necessarily related to numbers, members or diffusion. As Simonelli and Ferrarotti (1995) write, a minor sport can also have lot of athletes and followers, but it faces lot of difficulties to emerge.

As Rosner and Shropshire (2004) did, they identified four categories of niche sports. The first one are the minor league sports referring to those sports that do not represent the top level of competition, as for example the NBDL (National Basketball Development League) in US and the LND (Lega Nazionale Dilettanti) in Italy. The second category are the emerging sports which are representing the top level of their sports but are not receiving the same level of media coverage as mainstream sports enjoy (Greenhalgh, Simmons, Hambrick, and Greenwell, 2011). The third category is the indoor alternative to traditionally outdoor sport. The fourth category is the gender specific leagues, as for example WNBA (Women National Basket Association).

This attraction for the mass media generates a huge business that moves and sustains mainstream sports. Unlike mainstream sports, niche sports do not have the luxury of daily news coverage in the local and national newspaper sports sections. (Greenhalgh, Simmons, Hambrick, and Greenwell, 2011)

Although other disciplines can count a large number of athletes and followers, niche sports receive only a little space and in most of the cases it is insufficient for diffusing the news.

The only exception to this rule is the "big events", as for example the Olympic Games or the World Championships. They can provide a concentrated high attention but only for a limited time and when these events are over, in most of the cases minor sports are again immediately forgotten.

3.3 GENDER DIFFERENCES IN SPORT AND MASS MEDIA ATTENTION

As we saw during this chapter, the sport practise is generally considered to be the exaltation of the masculinity.

With the time some inequalities between genders disappeared but some other remain. Nowadays one of the most difficulties that women's sport must face is to find the right and appropriate way to attract mass media.

Connel (1987) writes that men tend to establish themselves throughout the sports that are considered to be competitive. For this reason women that enter the sport's world are seen as threats for the male's world.

Many research studies were conducted about the media constructions of gender, masculinity and femininity in sport and the most of the findings show that women receive much less media coverage than men.

After a research carried out in the year 1990 from the AAF (Amateur Athletic foundation of Los Angeles), Wenner (1998) declares that analyzing the sport's transmission for 6 weeks the result is that the news about male athletes were 92 %, while the news about female athletes were only 5% and the remaining 3% was about other arguments.

For example, we can take into consideration a famous American's sport magazine called *Sports Illustrated*. It is considered to be well known and respected for the quality of the sport contents. This magazine shows the annual *swimsuit issue*, that features top models wearing the latest styles in swim wear. The problem is that this issue portrays women as sex objects rather than as serious athletes and retrace the existing patterns of gender inequalities in sport and society.

As reported by Messner (2005) Between the years 1998 and 2000 only five women were present on the cover of the *Sport Illustrated* magazine.

Actually significant differences in the quality skills tend to underestimate women's performance, while men's shows and games are always seen under a particular and spectacular point of view.

Kane and Parks (1992) declare that the role of mass media is not only to diffuse news, but also to elaborate messages that should attract spectators, making them following the event with curiosity and active participation. As we can find written on the site of women soccer (www.womensoccer.com), many TV producers justify the little media coverage of women's sport declaring that the audience of sport's programs is composed from men that are not interested in the women's sport and for this reason they must give to the audience what the audience want.

Actually women's sports are considered to be a minority. As Whannel (2000) write, the research literature shows that the dominant media often shortchange women and minorities in sport. "They give them less airtime or print coverage than their higher-status counterparts, and when they cover women and minorities, they generally portray them with less respect and may even demean them in various obvious or not-so-obvious ways." (Howard, Nixon 2008)

A research analysis done by Messner, Dunbar and Hunt (2000), about the images of masculinity conveyed to U.S boys by the sport programms on television, shows that what actually broadcasted is "televised sports manhood formula". Some of the main themes are: (1)white males are the dominant authority figures; (2)sport is a male realm; (3)men dominate commercials and women appear only with men; (4)women are sex objects, props for men, or prizes for successful men.

Mainly, female athletes appear to be impoverished of their real image and often their agonistic aspect is underestimate.

3.4 WOMEN'S MOTIVATION TOWARD SPORT

Does the motivation toward sport really differ between genders?

On one hand, men tend to practise sport because they give lot of importance to the competition and personal ability. On the other hand women, tend to be stimulated by the socio-emotional factors as for example, fun and social interaction.

According to some research studies, women put more effort to be accepted rather than for having success. These motivations are more linked with the group and with the reaching of socio-emotional objectives rather than personal aims. The practise of sport for a woman has a double meaning. She wants to be socially accepted, which brings her to gain a social recognition of her skills and to increase the self-determination in front of the others.

So we can say that the dominant elements in the motivation toward sport for a girl are:

- a need of self-determination and of social recognition

- a need of achievement in a male's predominant field

ISTAT, the national institution of statistics in Italy, in the year 2000, conducted a study research on the motivations toward sports investigating about the differences between genders. From this study research emerged that men practise sport for passion and pleasure (70,1 %), for fun (51,8%), to be in shape (20,8 %). Subsequently came the possibility to come in touch with the nature (12,2 %) and for the values that the sport transmits (9,3 %).

If we look at the women, we can find another situation. The main motivations that push women toward sports are the need to be in shape (56,3 %), followed by the passion and pleasure (51,6 %) and for fun (46,8 %).

To make a little summary we can state that the motivations toward sport for women are the psychophysical health while for men the main motivations are passion and fun.

According to another study done by Fortier, Vallerand, Brière and Provencher (1995), women appear to be intrinsic motivated to reach the objectives and showed lower level of external regulation and of amotivation compared to men.

Chapter 4

Women's Football

Before starting speaking about Women's football, I would like to highlight that this sport can be seen as the symbol of the difficulty for women to enter the World of sports.

Although during the last years people seem to be more interested in this women's discipline, it faces still lot of difficulties to find adequate spaces and consensus. It is clear that when people think about Football, they imagine a game that consists in resistance, velocity and hard tackles and lot of physical effort. Consequently it is normally thought to be a male game, and in a certain way, this is right, but Women, as Trombino M. (1998) declares, demonstrated that Football could be also a female's game, especially because nowadays there is increased the tendency to focus more on tactical predisposition and on game's organisation, on which women pay lot of attention.

4.1 THE BIRTH OF WOMEN'S FOOTBALL

Where Women's football actually comes from is still a mystery as it is for many other sports, but what we surely know is that the birth of Women's football is thanks to the young women of the "Dick Kerr's Ladies" football team. During the First World War, because of the absence of the most of the male population, women had to do their job. It is right about here in the Dick Kerr munitions factory of Preston that was grounded the women's team called "Dick Kerr's Ladies". They used to train during the lunch or the breaks. This fact became interesting and many found-raising matches between the "Dick Kerr's Ladies" and male teams were organized.

As we can find write on the "Storia e Storie di calcio femminile" (Artemio Scardicchio, 2011), the success of these matches brought to the birth of many other women's football team, also out of England. The History tells us that during the year 1917 at Christmas time, the "Dick Kerr's Ladies" played against a French team in front of 25 thousand curious people.

Since 1921 the "Dick Kerr's Ladies" team received 121 invites to play and although they worked full-time in the factory, in that year they played 67 matches. The unexpected success gained by the "Dick Kerr's Ladies" worried the English Football Association that decided to stop the practise of Women's football. In the official statement there was written: "Complaints have been made as to football being played by women, the Council fell impelled to express their strong opinion that the game of football is quite unsuitable for females and ought not to be encouraged [...] the Council request the clubs belonging to the Association to refuse the use of their grounds for such matches." This measure retarded the development of women's football, but after the Second World War it began to expand reaching states like Germany, Norway and Sweden.

4.2 ITALIAN WOMEN'S FOOTBALL

The first information about Italian women's football date back to 1930, when was founded the first women's football group in Milan. (http://www.calciodonne.net)

A particular thing that used to distinguish Italian women's players from French, German and English women's players was the uniform. Italians used to wear the skirt while the others were wearing the same uniform as the one of the males.

In the year 1950,the Neapolitan baroness Angela Altini di Torralbo founded the Italian Women Football Association (Associazione Italiana Calcio Femminile, AICF). In the year 1959, took place a game between Rome and Naples and ended in a fight; this fact decided the end of AICF.

In the same years in Germany, England and Holland, Federations of male's football refused to give the fields to women's teams. In the year 1965, in the Milanese

Arena was played the match between Bologna and Inter. All the girls that were playing the game, were from Milan and the referee and coach of both teams was Miss. Valeria Rocchi. In the same year were born the societies of Genova and Giovani Viola of Florence.

The Italian Federation of Women Football (Federazione Italiana Calcio Femminile, FICF) was born in the year 1968 in Viareggio. The first Italian championship took place the same year and it consisted in two rounds (North and South) with five teams each. The first team that won the championship was the one of Genova, which won the game played in Pisa against the team of Roma.

In the year 1969, the FICF organized the European Cup. It was a four-team tournament and the teams participating were Italy, Denmark, France and England. The winner was Italy that beat Denmark with a score of 3-1.

The 31st of January 1970, ten societies left the FICF and signed the certificate of incorporation of the FIFGC (Federazione Italiana Femminile Giuoco Calcio). For the first time we can speak about the first league with an unique round of fourteen teams and the second league divided in four rounds for a total number of twenty four teams. Some norms about the memberships were established and the problem of the physical examination was taken into consideration.

In this period FICF and FIFGC organized two different Italian's championships with actually two winning teams. The FICF organized a World Cup inserting in the national team only the girls that were members of his Federation. The Denmark team won the World Cup in the final against Italy.

In the year 1972, thanks to the lawyer Giovanni Trabucco, FICF and FIFGC became a unique federation that was called FFIUGC (Federazione Femminile Italia Unita Giuoco Calcio) that after in the year 1986 took part of the FIGC (Federazione Italiana Giuoco Calcio).

With the help of the lawyer Giovanni Trabucco Women's football became more popular and year after year a federal structure took form with a president, two assistants president and presidents of the National League, Regional League and federal councillors. Were organized some national championships for the first and the second league, inter-regional third league and regional fourth league and some youth activities at provincial level and some tournaments.

In the year 1980 the Italian Women Football Association (Associazione Italiana Calciatrici) was established in Bergamo. This Association continued to operate until 1989 also in cooperation with the National Amateur League (Lega Nazionale Dilettanti, LND) and after some times it disappeared spontaneously. In the year 1983 female FIGC is recognized as joining the CONI receiving a little economic contribute.

In the year 1987 there is the nomination for Mr. Maurizio Forani as the first president of Women's football.

4.2.1 The current situation in Italy

Unfortunately nowadays in Italy Women's Football is not yet a professional game and although its popularity is increasing year after year, the passage to a professional game still remain a dream.

Nowadays women's football in Italy is part of the LND (Lega Nazionale Dilettanti), that leads the movement through the DCF (Divisione Calcio Femminile). The DFC manages the national championships of the premiere league and first division (Serie A, Serie A2 and Serie B). The second and third division (Serie C and Serie D) are handled by the Regional Committees, which are also part of LND.

During the year 2011 it was approved a reform that saw the increase of the teams playing in the premiere league (Serie A) from a number of 12 to 14. This change has been made to make the premiere league more interesting and more attractive for the media. As I already said the second and third division's championships are managed by the Regional Committees, which have a responsible person. Every region changes and also the person responsible change, obviously also the passion and the effort put in managing and developing this sport change. The worst situation we can find is in South Italy where there are some regions with only one team that must travel to another region to dispute a regular championship. Other than this way to operate from the person responsible, the clear differences from South and North of Italy can be connected with the economic difficulties of South Italy where results quite impossible to find out the sufficient resources to maintain alive a sport like women's football that is still considered to be a minor sport. Furthermore we must remember that the only few good infrastructure are always monopolized by male's teams.

I want only to spent few words about the problem of the infrastructures. Still they are property of the Communes, they should be available for both male and female teams. Actually these fields are often used by male teams and rarely it is permitted for women to play on its.

4.3 OUT OF EUROPE, the situation in USA

Dealing with women's football, we cannot forget to mention USA. The american team was the leader in this field.

The year 1991 took place the first official Women's World Cup in China with the triumph of U.S.A.

In the year 1999 The Women's World Cup was played in the U.S. This is saw as a turning point for the American's women football because with the victory of the U.S national team it brought lot of popularity to this game. Indeed U.S players signed contracts of million dollars with media and teams. After some years, in 2001, the WUSA was found (Women's United Soccer Association) and Women's Football became a professional sport.

The boom of women's players and the celebrity of this game allowed to think that could be the sport of the future in the U.S.

As we know, soccer (football) in the U.S is not considered to be a major sport. The great performance of the USA team in the WWC and the gained huge success of some players as Brandi Chastain and Mia Hamm let think about a soccer revolution. Not only for the popularity and the expansion of the discipline itself but also because women's soccer was considered to be more interesting and developed as male's soccer.

Unfortunately after some years the popularity of women's football seems to decrease. The media attention after the big boom in the 1999, has strongly declined and the WUSA and the other professional and semi-professional leagues must face lot of money problems.

In a recent article, Noah Davis (2010), quotes Scott French, a journalist who covered the women's game for two decades: "There was a perception in 1999 and 2000 that women's soccer was more popular than men's soccer, but it was never true. That team was popular. That event [the '99 World Cup] was popular. Mia was popular. But women's soccer was never more popular than the men's game."

This declaration shows as a recurring rule that a women's sport cannot have much more popularity and consideration than a men's sport.

4.4 WOMEN'S FOOTBALL AND MASS MEDIA

Football is known as a king sport for mass media. It is played everywhere and in its every forms. " Globally, football is played in more than 200 countries and in many countries is the most popular spectator sport, for both live and mediated audiences" (Nicholson, 2007).

This sport has become popular also among poorer countries because it results easy to play; only a ball and an open space are required.

Dealing with male's football, we can notice how this sport has gained lot of attention from the mass media. In Italy for example, mass media tend to focus only on male's football forgetting and laying aside other sports. The predominance of football is clearly found in every single media tools; for example the sport's section of any newspaper is dominated by football.

It can sound as an absurdity, but women's football does not have the same media attention and coverage. Actually in the recent years, thanks also to the development of new media as Internet and the social networks, women's football experiences a little increasing interest.

The point is that compared to men's football, the women's one lays in almost total absence of media interest and attention. Nevertheless men dominate the football's world in the media and it appears very difficult to undermine these types of prejudices.

Something should and can be made to change this situation but has to come from the heart, from the inside. I really hope that the communication media tools in the future will become aware of women's football considering it not as particular delegation of football but a real and independent discipline. The crucial point is to understand that men and women play a game that is the same, but it differs because of the natural differences between genders. There are not pre-established inequalities but simple natural differences that must be understood and taken into consideration.

In my opinion, this concept must be assimilated to allow women's football to emerge.

Chapter 5

Research objectives and methodology

Sport has become a strong and powerful mechanism able to connect people. During the last decades many researchers conducted lot of studies in order to investigate the Sport's World. What do we actually have now are lot of interesting findings in different sport's field. When I had to decide my thesis' topic I did a little investigation on the motivations toward the practise of sport. Because I could not find too much works related to this topic, I found very stimulating to try to better look into it.

My research wants to investigate the motivations that push female athletes toward the practise of sport. In particular I wanted to understand what are the main motivations for women football players. It wants also to understand the lacks and the difficulties faced by women's football to emerge, trying to delineate an overview about the future perspectives. My analysis has been done through the collection of quantitative data with the help of questionnaires and qualitative data with an interview to a person directly involved in the women's football world.

My thesis starts with the review of literature about sport motivation. I found out two very interesting theories, self-determinant theory and achievement goal theory, and the sport motivation scale on which we can measure the type and efficacy of motivations. A paragraph is also dedicated to the influence that peers, coaches and parents have on the sport motivation. Than come women's sport and in particular the inequalities between genders, the hard relationship with the mass media and the difficulties faced by women's sport to emerge. After that I develop a paragraph on the motivation of women toward sport. This will be followed by the analysis of the specific case of women's football.

5.1 RESEARCH OBJECTIVES

1) The first research objective of my thesis is to find out what are the factors that initially and currently push women players in the practise of football. On the basis of the two theories (AGT and SDT) and the sport motivation scale, developed and explained in the literature review, I will be able to understand the type and the efficacy of the main motivations.

2) The second research objective of my thesis is to understand what are the lacks and what could be the crucial points for the development of women's football from the athlete's point of view.

3) The third objective of my research is to define specific characteristics of different groups of women football players.

5.2 SAMPLING

The research was addressed only to women football players from all over the world, in order to investigate the motivations toward the practise of football and to understand the level of information about women's football and the perceptions about it. In particular it was designed for Italian women football players. Though, I decided to formulate two questionnaires, one in English and one in Italian, because I wanted to collect the forms from other countries to have an international view. The persons who full filled the questionnaires were almost all from Italy. I noticed that fortunately the persons, who answer the questionnaire, came from all the Italian regions so I could have a real good national view. In order to have a better explanation on the perception of women's football I interviewed Roberto Genta, which is involved in the women's football world since many years.

5.3 DATA COLLECTION

The research began with the creation of the questionnaires in March 2011. In order to reach as much persons as I could, I created the questionnaires online. They remained online from the end of March 2011 till the beginning of June 2011. In order to spread its, I used the major social network visiting the most important women's football pages and posting the link on their wall. I used this system for the English questionnaire, while with the one in Italian I used my contacts in the women's football world to reach girls from all the Italian regions. Moreover I could rely upon my friends, which play football, who forward the link of the questionnaire to their football player friends. After one month I noticed that using the social network was not sufficient to reach the international sphere, so I sent some email directly to the most important clubs of Germany and USA but with no responses. At the end I collected 185 questionnaires; 177 filled by Italian football players and only 8 by players from other countries. Furthermore I prepared an interview for Roberto Genta composed by 9 questions about the women's football world.

5.4 SURVEY INSTRUMENTS

5.4.1 Questionnaire

The questionnaire was produced to investigate the motivations of women players toward the practice of football and to understand the perception and information about women's football. It is composed of 17 questions divided into 3 main parts. Different question types were employed as for example Yes/No type and Likert-scale. About this last type of question the respondents were asked to express their opinion regarding some statements using a scale from 1 to 4 where "1" is "Not important at all" and "4" is "Very important". I made the decision to not insert the choice "I do not know", in order to avoid the possibility to have invalid questionnaires.

The questionnaire begins with the questions about how long has the athlete been playing football and since when does she play football. For the English questionnaire there are two more questions asking if in her country is women's football a professional game and then if she is a professional player. The first part wants to investigate the personal motivations that initially and then currently push the female athletes toward the practise of football. These two questions are developed on a base of a Likert scale from 1 (not important at all) to 4 (very important). The question about the factors that initially influence the athlete in the practise of football has 10 statements. One the basis of the SMS, the Sport Motivation Scale, I decided the more appropriate statements that could be related to a specific type of motivation developed by Deci and Ryan (1985). As I already wrote in the literature review, The Sport Motivation Scale, consists of seven subscales that measure three types of Intrinsic Motivation (IM to Know, IM to Accomplish Things, and IM to Experience Stimulation), three forms of regulation for Extrinsic Motivation (Identified, Introjected, and External), and Amotivation.

I took as example a questionnaire created by Pelletier, Brière, Vallerand, Tuson and Blais (1995) constituted with the aim to explore the sport motivation of some athletes practising different sports. Naturally during the creation of these questions I took into consideration also the Task and Ego Orientation in Sport Questionnaire (TEOSQ; Duda, 1989), able to catch individual differences in motivational orientations in AGT. This instrument contains a 7-item task orientation and a 6-item ego orientation. Responses were recorded on a 5-point Likert scale with "strongly disagree" scored as 1 and "strongly agree" scored as 5. Using this questionnaire lot of studies were conducted in order to examine various arguments about sport motivation as for example the motivational orientation in youth sport participation (Cindy H.P. Sit, Koenraad J. Lindner, 2005; Sean P. Cumming, Ronald E. Smith, Frank L. Smoll, Martyn Standage, Joel R. Grossbard, 2008; Maarten Vansteenkiste , Lennia Matos, Willy Lens, Bart Soenens, 2007)

So actually my intention was to understand if women's football players are more intrinsic or extrinsic motivated and if there is the tendency to be more task or ego oriented.

The second part of the questionnaire is about the perceptions of women's football from the athlete's point of view. It is composed of 5 questions. The first question deals with the possibility to continue to practise football in 3, 5, or more than 5 years. It is also a question based on a Likert-scale. The other question, also a Likert scale, is about how important is football in the athlete's life. I created these two questions to better understand the influence and the importance that a sport like football can have in the athletes' everyday's life.

Following comes the question related to the development of women's football. I asked what does she think that could help this sport to become more popular. I gave 7 statements with a Likert scale from 1 to 4. The next question I put, is formulated to know how much and if every athlete is actually informed about her sport. It is a Yes/No answer question type about the Women's Football World Cup.

5.4.2 Interview

In order to investigate the perception and the development of women's football, I decided to interview Roberto Genta. I met Roberto in Verona in April 2011 to do my interview. He is now employed as journalist for the Website *calciodonne.it.* He works in the field since he was 24 years old. Initially he started as goalkeepers' trainer than he became the coach of some youth teams up to the women's premiere league. He always worked in the marketing field trying to give to the women's football world as much visibility as possible working together with Television and Radio. I structured the interview in 9 questions and I choose to concentrate on the perception, the expectations, the changes and the problematic of women's football in Italy.

5.5 STATISTICAL ANALYSIS

Once the questionnaires were collected and an Excel table were formed, the data were ready to be analyzed. In order to conduce a better elaboration of the data and a more precise statistical analysis, I decided to use SPSS.

The elaboration of the collected data started with the descriptive analysis of the responses given in the questionnaires.

Concerning this part, specific statistical indexes were used to provide a first descriptive investigation:

- Arithmetical average
- Median
- Percentage
- Mode

In order to get a deeper analysis and to value and elaborate the different variables, some statistical methods were used.

Chapter 6

Analysis of the results

Before starting with the analysis of the results, I wish to remember that my questionnaire was directed only to women football players. Actually it was a little bit difficult to find lot of girls playing football. However, Thanks to the social networks and to my friends, I was able to collect 185 complete questionnaires. Moreover it was even more difficult to reach girls out of Italy and for this reason the majority of the respondents (95%) is form Italy as showed by the *Figure 1*, and the remaining come from Germany (3%), USA (1%) and Israel (1%). After the collection of all the questionnaires, I used SPSS in order to create the statistics and Figure very useful for the elaboration and interpretation of the results.

Figure 1: Nationality

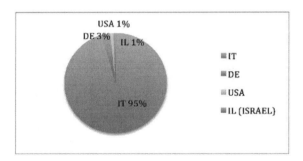

Now I want to begin my analysis trying to give a sociological profile of the interviewees. To outline who is the type of person answering the questionnaire I analyzed the results of the last part of my questionnaire. As said before, the majority comes from Italy. *Figure 2* shows that 84% of the respondents are from the North of Italy. More precisely a relevant part comes from Verona 14,6%, from Bozen 11,9% and from Padova 6,5%.

Figure 2: Italian proveniences

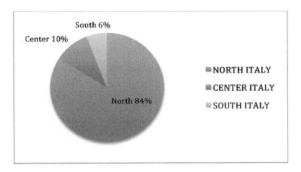

The reason of such a high number of respondents coming from northern Italy lies in the fact that I played football in three different societies in Veneto and in Südtirol. As consequence the most of my friends come from these regions.

Figure 3 offers an overview of the age of the respondents and the respective frequencies. The x-axis indicates the age of the interviewees while the y-axis indicates the frequencies. So what appears is that there are some evident peaks. The highest percentage is represented by the 18 years old where the frequency is 21 that corresponds to 11,4% of the total, than there is another peak indicating the 21 years old where the frequency is 17 that is 9,2% and the last is the 24 years old, with the frequency 18 that is 9,7%. The median of the ages is 23 years old.

Figure 3: Age of the respondents

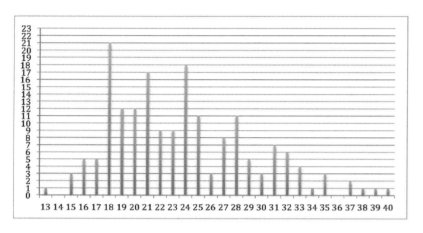

Figure 4 shows how many of the respondents began playing football at that determinate age. The x-axis highlights the age since when girls are playing football, while y-axis represent the frequencies. It is clear that the majority began in between 6 - that is the highest peak – and 14 years old. The calculated median is 11 years old.

Figure 4: Age and frequencies about the beginning of playing football

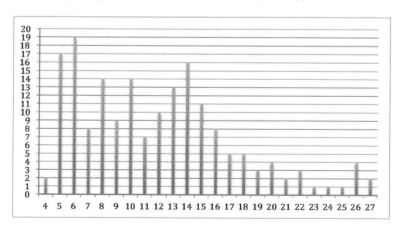

From the results obtained by analyzing the age of the respondents, what shows *Figure 5* here under could be expected.

Figure 5: Respondents' employment

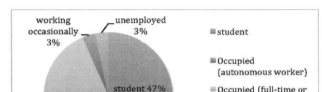

The majority of the women playing football is student (47%) and the other majority works as full-time or part-time employee. What appears further is that 92% are single and 99% have no children. Furthermore 43% have the college diploma, 26% university degree, 17% have the middle diploma, 7% the vocational diploma while only 7% achieved the postgraduate diploma. 2% have no title.

To make more interesting the delineation of the profile are the results from the question "how much important is football in your daily life", a Likert-scale from 1 to 4 was used, where 1 was "not important at all" and 4 was "very important". The results are presented in *Figure 6*. There are two relevant evident outcomes. 43 % of the respondents consider football to be "very important" (4) in their everyday life and another 43% gave 3 that is just under the mark "very important". Interesting to see is that only 1% of the respondents consider football to be "not important at all". The mean value is 3,29.

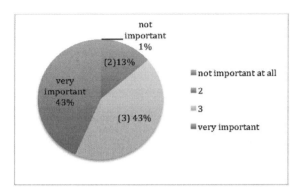

Considering the fact that this questionnaire was directed only to women playing football, I found also interesting to ask in which category they play. This question can help me further to understand if there are some interactions with motivations toward sport or in the perception of women's football. As *Figure 7* shows, three-fourths of the respondents play in the premiere league (25%), first division (23%) and second division (28%). The remaining piece of the pie chart is occupied by the percentages of the youth team 11%, third division 5% and only 8% are playing in any category.

Figure 7: Football categories

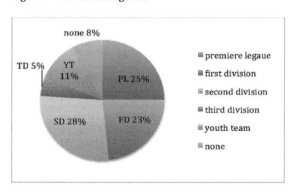

In order to understand the family background of the respondents a question about sport activities of the parents was introduced. *Figure 8* shows the percentage of the interviewees having at least one parent playing or that has been playing at a competitive level any kind of sport. The 60% answered yes, while 40% answered no.

Figure 8: Parent playing or that played sport at competitive level

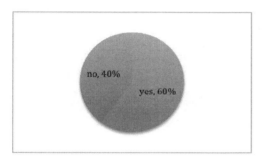

Thanks to the results obtained until now I can delineate a general profile of the respondent. The typical respondent is from the north of Italy, she is 23 years old and began playing football at 11 years old. She currently plays in the second division. She is student and single and one of her parents has been playing at a competitive level.

The results that I am going to analyze now are part of the series of questions that want to investigate the motivations that push women toward the practise of football.

The most important way I found out to help me in this aim is to develop two different questions; one is about the factors that initially influenced the ladies in the choice of practise football, showed in the *Figure 9*; the other one is about the factors that currently push the respondents in the practise of football, showed in the *Figure 10*. Both questions are formulated on a Likert-scale from 1 (not important at all) to 4 (very important).

Some factors that I chose are used to understand the type and efficacy of motivations that has been investigated on the basis of the SMS, AGT and SDT; while other factors are used to investigate specific aspects of the motivations. Thanks to these two questions I am able now to delineate a motivational profile for my interviewees.

I would like to start my analysis with the question about the initial factors influencing the choice of playing football. On the basis of AGT and SDT I created some specific factors. "My parents influenced me" and "my teachers at school influenced me" can be connected with the *External Regulation* that is a part of Extrinsic Motivation (EM). The factor "sport is important for the maintenance and development of a healthy body" can be connected to *Identification* that is also part of EM.

"My friends used to play" and "to find new friends" are factors that can be related with social motivation. This is one of the most important and easy motivation found that push generally people in beginning a sport activity.

"There was a team in the neighbourhood" and "the city offered good infrastructures" these two motivations show merely that the convenience of team in the nearby and the awareness to have good infrastructures can be a really strong factor to begin the practise of sport discipline. I made the choice to insert also two more factors that are "I used to watch the football matches on TV" and "I used to watch live matches at the stadium/arena". I thought about the possibility to be influenced by the show of the game itself and also by the heroes that play every Sunday at the stadium. This could be a probable motivation to start playing football. Everyone wants to emulate his/her idol, especially kids.

So now looking at *Figure 9*, it represents the mean average about this specific question, obtained from all the questionnaires. These results show us that the main factors initially pushing girls toward the practise of football are "I used to watch football matches in TV" with the highest average rate of 2,8, followed by "sport is important for the maintenance and development of a healthy body" (2,58) and "there was a team in the neighbourhood" (2,25). The factors "my brother/father plays/ used to play football" and "to find new friends" have an average rate of 2,02. Following, there are "I used to watch the live matches at the stadium/arena" with 1,99 and "my friends used to play" with 1,98. Actually it is a little bit surprising to me because I would rather expect higher rates coming with factors "to find new friends" or "my friends used to play" that are representing social motivations. It is also interesting to notice that the influence of the teachers has the lowest average rate 1,2 and the push of parents is only 1,63. It means that neither social motivations nor the push from the parents or teachers had a strong relevance.

So summarising the results we can say that girls are pushed more by the desire to emulate football idols, and the convenience represented by having a team in the neighbourhood. Moreover because of the high rate of the factor "sport is important for the maintenance and development of a healthy body" that can be related to *Identification*, a specific type of EM, we can state that female athletes are also extrinsic motivated to begin the practise of football.

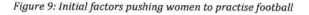

Figure 9: Initial factors pushing women to practise football

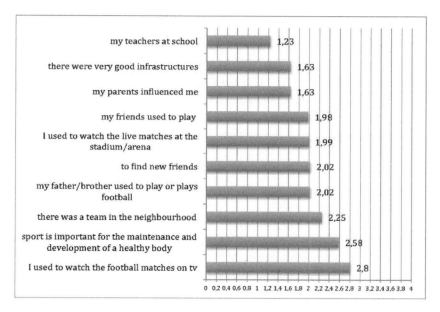

Let me now analyse the factors that currently push women toward the practise of football. During the creation of these factors I decided to use some new aspects and some of the previous question.

A factor that I took from the previous question is the social aspect expressed by the sentence "socialize with my friends" that can also be a relevant motivation to continue the practise of a sport.

Moreover I insert also the element "be in shape" that can be associated in a certain way with the sentence of the previous question "sport is important for the maintenance and development of a healthy body".

On the basis of AGT and SDT I create the factors "the pleasure felt during matches " and "the pleasure felt playing ". They could be seen as two very similar questions, but actually there is a subtle difference that I am going to explain now. "The pleasure felt playing" is related to *Intrinsic Motivation* (IM) *to experience stimulation* that means to practise a certain sport activity in order to experience stimulating experiences. Actually with this factor we must also state that id connected with *task orientation* that is part of the AGT, *Achievement Goal Theory.* It expresses the tendency to learn new skills and play without looking at the others, but only at himself. Naturally also the factor "the pleasure felt during matches" can be related to *Intrinsic Motivation to experience stimulation* but it can also express a way to show personal skills by competing against the opponent. For this reason, this factor can also be connected with *ego orientation* that is part of the AGT.

Interesting to notice is that AGT and SDT are in a certain way connected each other. While speaking about *task orientation,* that is part of AGT, we can state that is a way to learn new skills, improve himself without looking at the others. These could be signals of an internal motivation that is properly *Intrinsic Motivation* (SDT).

"The pleasure while mastering difficult techniques" is directly connected with *IM toward accomplishment.* The activities are done to experience satisfaction in mastering difficult techniques. So as said before, the desire to improve himself and learn new skills can be connected also with *task orientation.*

The element "the coach pushes me" is similar to the factors "my parents influenced me" and "my teachers at school". They are all related with *External Regulation,* so mainly a motivation toward an activity that comes from the external, by the push of someone else, and not from the person itself.

Other two factors that I put in this question – "to become a professional player" and "develop aspects of my character" – are related to Extrinsic Motivation in specific to *Identification.* It refers to a way athletes can grow up and develop as persons. Actually "to become a professional player" can also have an *ego-oriented* connotation. It wants to express the competition with others and being better than the others.

Remaining in the SDT context I used the sentence "not any more motivation" to express the other aspect that appears in the Theory with *Intrinsic Motivation* and *Extrinsic Motivation,* which is *Amotivation.* When a person is neither intrinsically nor extrinsically motivated is amotivated. It can happen that a person is doing an activity such as playing football but he is actually not motivated.

The next two factors that I am going to analyse are connected with the demand of being a woman playing a typical male game. "Show to men that also girls can play football" and "share a common identity". Dealing with the latter factor, it refers to a way for women football players to share something that is present only in the women's football environment. This happens over all for minor sports. As we will see in *Discussion and conclusions,* event like FIFA WWC, can represent not only an opportunity to play and promote a minor sport like women's football, but also a way through which the players can share a common identity; it is a sort of "way to be" only shared and recognized by those playing that particular game.

As underlined in the Literature review, for long time male has dominated sport, fortunately nowadays the situation is a little bit changed but still lot can be done to reach the equilibrium. "Show to men that also girls can play football" is a factor that can express the willingness of women to demand their identity in sport also at high level.

The factors remaining do not deal with the Theories expressed till now. They are "passion" and "addiction" that are two instinctive elements. For this reason it is really hard to find out a specific explanation that could help us to analyze and understand what there is behind them.

Figure 10: Current factors pushing women to practise football

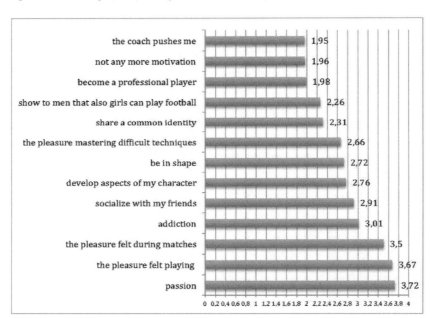

Figure 10 shows the results obtained from the Likert-scale question about the factors that currently push women players toward the practise of football. The main factor is "passion" with 3,72 of mean average. If we compare the higher mean average of the previous question we can notice that it was only 2,8, it means that passion is the most and really important factor. As said before there is no explanation behind this factor, it is instinctive and simple. Women football players are mainly pushed by passion toward the practise of their sport.

Then come with a mean average of 3,67 "the pleasure felt playing" and with 3,5 "the pleasure felt during matches". As underlined in the previous lines, they are similar but not identical factors. Both are representing *Intrinsic Motivation* (IM) *to experience stimulation*.

If we go further in the analysis of the first three factors showed in *Figure 10*, we can notice that despite what happened for the question about the initial factors, this question obtained higher scores of the mean averages.

To underline this fact, I analyzed in specific the first three factors, which obtained the higher scores, "passion", "the pleasure felt playing" and "the pleasure felt during matches".

As we can see in *Figure 11*, which represent the factor "passion", 80% of the interviewees consider it to be "very important", while only 2% think it is "not important at all".

Let's make a comparison between the two factors that obtained the highest score of mean average "passion" (current push) and "I used to watch football matches on TV" (initial push). As shown by *Figure 11* and *Figure 12*, it is surprising to see that only 30% of the respondents consider "I used to watch football matches on TV" to be "very important" and there is a huge 14% that consider it as "not important at all".

Figure 11: Passion

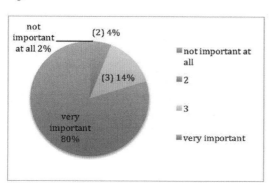

Figure 12: I used to watch the football matches on TV (initial factor)

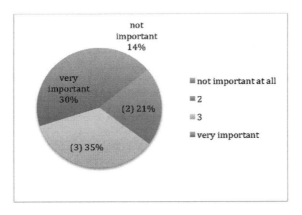

I also want to go further in the analysis of the factors "the pleasure felt playing" and "the pleasure felt during matches". For the first factor, as visible in *Figure 13*, there is 73% of interviewees considering it as "very important", but actually more interesting too see is that nobody (0%) consider is as "not important at all".

Focusing on the other factor, "pleasure felt during matches", there is also a relevant percentage, 65% rating this factor with the higher score (4) and only 2% rating it with the lowest (1).

Figure 13: Pleasure felt playing

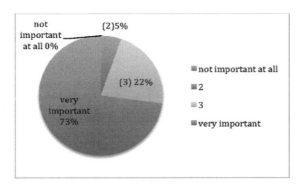

Figure 14: Pleasure felt during matches

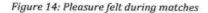

Figure 14: Pleasure felt during matches

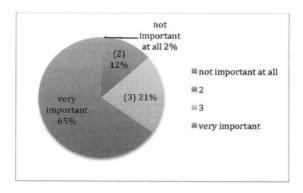

After that we find "addiction" with a mean average of 3,01. As "passion" it is a factor that could not easily be explained, measured and they vary across different persons.

With a mean average of 2,91 there is "socialize with my friend". If we look further, we can notice that 29% of the interviewees consider being very important the factor "socialize with my friends" while only 9% consider "find new friend" as relevant element to begin the practise of football.

Figure 15: Initial push, score of "to find new friends"

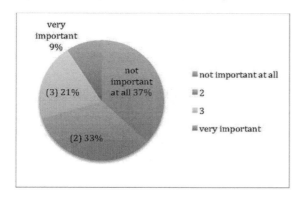

Figure 16: Current push, score of "socialize with my friends"

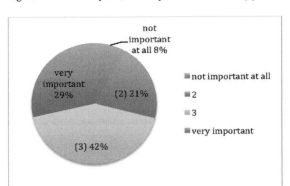

"Develop aspects of my character" has a mean average of 2,76, followed by "be in shape" with 2,72. Than comes "the pleasure mastering difficult techniques" with 2,66 that is representing *IM toward accomplishment* and *task orientation.*

"Share a common identity" and "show to men that also girls can play football" have obtained a mean average of 2,66 and 2,31. They represent the demand of being a girl playing a typical male game.

The last three factors in the mean average rank are "become a professional player" with 1,98 than "not any more motivation" with 1,96 and "the coach pushes me" with 1,95.

So to summarize the results we can say that girls are currently mainly pushed by passion in the practise of their sport, football. Because of the high mean average of "pleasure felt playing" and "pleasure felt during matches" we can state that girls are also intrinsic motivated (to experience stimulation) to continue the practise of football. However there is an influence of both *task and ego orientation.*

Interesting to notice in that "the coach pushes me" obtained the lowest score; even lower than "not any more motivation" that represents *Amotivation.* So it means that there is no external push for the practise of this sport.

A little bit surprising is that the demand of being a woman playing a typical male game is not a relevant factor as shown from the results of "share a common identity" (2,31) and "show men that also girls can play football" (2,26).

In this research I did not only want to understand the present and the past situation of the players, but also the future perspectives. For this reason I decided to investigate how probable is to continue the practise of football in the next 3, 5 and more than 5 years.

Figure 17: Probability in the next 3 years

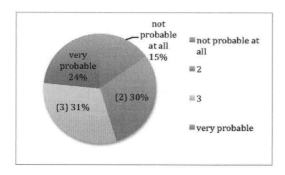

Figure 18: Probability in the next 5 years

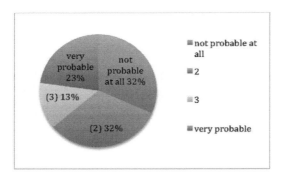

Figure 17, Figure 18 and *Figure 19* are obtained by asking the question – how much probable it is to continue to practise football in the next three years, five years and more than five years? - .

As shown by the *Figure 17*, the 50% of the girls interviewed consider very probable to continue the practise of football within 3 years while only 7% consider it not probable at all.

Figure 18 highlights that 24% consider very probable to continue the practise of football within 5 years but also a 15 % consider it not probable at all.

The last Figure, *Figure 19*, shows the results about the possibility to continue the practise of football in more than five years. Only 23% think it is very probable, while a huge 32% think that is not probable at all.

Interesting to notice is that there is quite high level of uncertainty in long-term future, while there is the tendency to be more aware about the short-term future.

Going further with the years we can see that there is a decrease of the percentage of people thinking very probable to continue playing football and an increased percentage of people thinking not probable at all to continue the practise of football.

Figure 20: Factors that could help the development of women's football

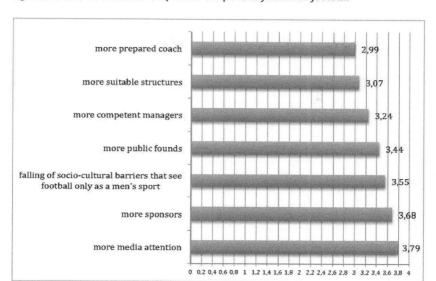

Figure 20 shows the results obtained by asking the question – what do you think can help women's football becoming a more popular and developed sport? – It is a question based on a Likert-scale from 1 to 4 with seven factors.

With this question I wanted to investigate the athletes' perception about the possibilities of development of women's football. Actually the question is, on what do we have to focus more in order to see a relevant progression of this sport?

Every single factor obtained a really high score because every of them could all be very important. Naturally I was aware of this fact but my aim was to understand which are the most important from the athletes' point of view.

The most rated factor, shown by the *Figure 20,* is "more media attention" with a mean average of 3,79. As underlined in the Literature review, the media attention can say a lot about the popularity and development of a sport. The media attention generates a huge business that can move and sustain a sport; of course this is not the case of women's football that receive only a little space that is insufficient for diffusing the news.

The other factor that received a relevant score is "more sponsors" with a mean average rate of 3,68. As we all know, sponsors are one of the main mechanisms that allow sports to be alive. Sponsors give money and technical material that is essential for the maintenance and development of the teams but also for sport events. Solid and reliable sponsors represent the basis for the development of a sport. What if sports were deprived of sponsors?

Another relevant factor that received 3,55 mean average is "falling of socio-cultural barriers that see football only as a men's sport". Actually the gender inequality is still a problem that every woman's sport must face. Especially for football that is the male's game par excellence.

The other factors, receiving the lowest score as shows *Figure 20* are "more public founds" with 3,44, "more competent managers " 3,24, "more suitable structures" 3,07 and "more prepared coach" 2,99.

Figure 21: Did you know about the FIFA Women's World Cup?

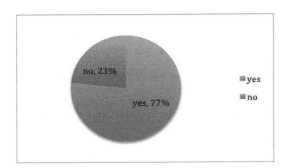

Figure 21, shows the percentages resulted by asking the question – Did you know about the FIFA Women's World Cup? -.

I decided to insert also this question in order to understand how much informed are the interviewees about their sport. I have to explain that during summer 2011, the FIFA Women's World Cup (WWC) takes place in Germany. For this reason I found interesting to investigate if they really know about it, especially out of Germany.

The result indicate that 77% knew about the FIFA WWC while only 23% did not know about it. Actually this must be a really good result showing a high percentage of girls that knows about the FIFA WWC, but if we think about the meaning and the dimensions of this type of event, it appears incredible to me that there is a huge 23% of women players that did not know about this event.

Obviously the reason why can be connected to the fact that women's football players are not highly interested in following their sport at an international level. However we must still remember that for a sport like this, there is too much little information and too low media attention that do not permit a relevant flow of news.

Figure 22: Factors brought by the FIFA Women's World Cup

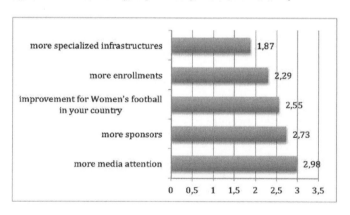

The last question that I want to analyse is about what the athletes think the WWC will bring to Women's football. I decided few important factors that have been scored on a Likert-scale from 1 to 4. This question is interesting because it allows me to understand the perception about the possibilities of a big event such as WWC to bring some improvements.

The results of *Figure 22* indicate that "more media attention" is the factor that gained the highest mean average with 2,98. Than comes "more sponsors" with an average rate of 2,73 followed by "improvement for women's football in your country" with 2,55. The last two factors with a lower score are "more enrolments" with 2,29 and "more specialized infrastructures" with 1,87.

Actually these findings match perfectly with the previous question about the essential factors that can help women's football to become a more developed sport. On the basis of these results we can state that the FIFA WWC should bring exactly what is needed by women's football to begin a good development.

Going further, it is interesting to make a more specific investigation. I wanted to understand if there is a relationship of dependence between some variables. In order to reach my aim I used SPSS and I conducted χ^2 tests.

The variables used in the χ^2 test were "Did you know about the FIFA WWC?" and the statements about which factors are needed to improve women's football. This is made in order to investigate whether girls who know about the FIFA WWC have different ideas than those not being aware of the FIFA WWC of the factors necessarily for the women's football development.

I created a cross tabulation for every single statement in relation to the question about the FIFA WWC. From the results obtained, there are only two χ^2 tests that are significant [$\rho < 0,05$]. The other tests are not significant, so there is no relationship between the variables.

The first significant test refers to the cross tabulation, showed in *Table 1*, that takes into consideration the awareness of the FIFA WWC and the factor "more competent managers". The χ^2 test shows that there is a significant relationship [at $p < 0,05$] between the variables [$\chi^2=14,827$ and $p= 0,002$].

The results show that 54,9% of the persons that know about the FIFA WWC consider the factor "more competent managers" to be "very important" for the development of women's football. While only 28,6% of persons that do not know about the FIFA WWC consider that factor to be "very important".

The 2,8% of people knowing about the FIFA WWC consider the factor "more competent managers" to be "not important at all", while if we look at the people answering "no" about the FIFA WWC, we can notice that there is a huge 9,5% considering that factor to be "not important at all".

Table 1: Relationship between the variables Awareness of the FIFA WWC and the factor "more competent managers"

			more competent managers				
			Not important at all	2	3	Very important	Total
Do you know about the FIFA WWC ?	yes	Count	4	24	36	78	142
		% within do you know about FIFA WWC?	2.8%	16.9%	25.4%	54.9%	100.0%
	no	Count	4	5	21	12	42
		% within do you know about FIFA WWC?	9.5%	11.9%	50.0%	28.6%	100.0%
Total		Count	8	29	57	90	184
		% within do you know about FIFA WWC?	4.3%	15.8%	31.0%	48.9%	100.0%

The other χ^2 test that is significant refers to the cross tabulation, showed in *Table 2*, that put into relationships the awareness of the FIFA WWC and "more suitable structures". The χ^2 test shows that there is a significant relationship [at p< 0,05] between the variables [χ^2= 9,244; p= 0,026].

The 41,1% of those who know about the FIFA WWC, they perceive the factor "more suitable structures" as "important" (rated with "3"). While if we consider the awareness of the FIFA WWC, there is a 35,7% that perceive the same factor as "not important" (rated with "2").

Table 2: Relationship between the variables Awareness of the FIFA WWC and the factor "more suitable structures"

			more suitable structures				
			not important at all	2	3	very important	Total
Do you know about FIFA WWC?	yes	Count	6	23	58	54	141
		% within do you know about the FIFA WWC?	4.3%	16.3%	41.1%	38.3%	100.0%
	no	Count	3	15	10	14	42
		% within do you know about the FIFA WWC?	7.1%	35.7%	23.8%	33.3%	100.0%
Total		Count	9	38	68	68	183
		% within do you know about the FIFA WWC?	4.9%	20.8%	37.2%	37.2%	100.0%

The other relationship, showed in *Table 3*, that I want to take into consideration is that one between the "initial push of the teachers" and "more prepared coaches" as factor for the development of women's football. The 34,8% of persons that consider the initial push of the teachers as "not important at all" think that "more prepared coaches " is an important factor in order to develop women's football.

Table 3: Relationship between the variables "Initial push of the teachers" and "more prepared coaches"

			more prepared coaches				
			not important at all	2	3	very important	Total
initial push of the teachers	not important at all	Count	10	41	55	52	158
		% within initial push from teachers	6,3%	25,9%	34,8%	32,9%	100,0%
	2	Count	0	1	5	9	15
		% within initial push from teachers	,0%	6,7%	33,3%	60,0%	100,0%
	3	Count	1	3	0	2	6
		% within initial push from teachers	16,7%	50,0%	,0%	33,3%	100,0%
	very important	Count	0	0	2	3	5
		% within initial push from teachers	,0%	,0%	40,0%	60,0%	100,0%
Total		Count	11	45	62	66	184
		% within initial push from teachers	6,0%	24,5%	33,7%	35,9%	100,0%

Now, if we take into consideration the two variables, "current push of coaches" and "more prepared coaches", as shown in *Table 4*, the cross tabulation appears to be similar. The 42,9% of people considering "not important at all" the current push of coaches think that "more prepared coaches" is a very important factor for the development of women's football.

Table 4: Relationship between the variables "current push of the coaches" and "more prepared coaches"

			more prapared coaches				
			not important at all	2	3	very important	Total
current push from coaches	not important at all	Count	6	16	18	30	70
		% within current push form coaches	8,6%	22,9%	25,7%	42,9%	100,0%
	2	Count	3	20	19	23	65
		% within current push form coaches	4,6%	30,8%	29,2%	35,4%	100,0%
	3	Count	1	7	19	7	34
		% within current push form coaches	2,9%	20,6%	55,9%	20,6%	100,0%
	very important	Count	1	2	5	6	14
		% within current push form coaches	7,1%	14,3%	35,7%	42,9%	100,0%
Total		Count	11	45	61	66	183
		% within current push form coaches	6,0%	24,6%	33,3%	36,1%	100,0%

Actually the χ^2 of both cross tabulation appears to be not significant. For the first one is [χ^2= 13,066; p= 0,160] and for the second one is [χ^2= 13,556; p= 0,139].

The χ^2 are not significant [should $p< 0,05$], so there is no relationship between the variables.

Finally I created three cross tabulations in order to analyse if there is a relationship between the persons who are students and the probability for them to continue the practise of football in the next three, five and more than five years.

First of all it is important to state that 47% of the total respondents are students, while the others are 53%. So it appears clear that the majority of the interviewees is student.

Figure 23: Students and Others

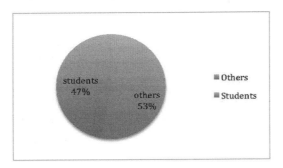

Table 5 puts into relationship the "Students"/ "Others" and the probability to continue the practise of football in the next three years. The 48,8% of the students consider "very probable" to continue playing football in the next three years while only 6,1% of them think it "not probable at all". Actually the χ^2 test shows that there is not a significant relationship between the variables as [χ^2= 6,753; p= 0,080].

Table 5: Relationship between the variables "Students-Others" and "probability to continue football in the next three years"

			prob. to continue football in the next 3 years				
			not probable at all	2	3	very probable	Total
Others (0) – Students (1)	0	Count	7	18	21	49	95
		% within Others – Students	7,4%	18,9%	22,1%	51,6%	100,0%
	1	Count	5	7	30	40	82
		% within Others – Students	6,1%	8,5%	36,6%	48,8%	100,0%
Total		Count	12	25	51	89	177
		% within Others – Students	6,8%	14,1%	28,8%	50,3%	100,0%

Table 6 shows the relationship between the students and the probability of playing football in five years. The percentages change a little bit, there is a small decrease of the students considering "very probable" to continue the practise of football which are 24,4%, while the students considering it "not probable at all" are a little bit increased till 8,5%. As it happened for the previous one, also here the χ^2 test shows that there is not a significant relationship between the variables, $[\chi^2= 6,057; p= 0,109]$.

Table 6: Relationship between the variables "Students-Others" and "probability to continue football in the next five years"

			prob. to continue football in the next five years				
			not probable at all	2	3	very probable	Total
Others (0) – Students (1)	0	Count	20	28	25	22	95
		% within Others – Students	21,1%	29,5%	26,3%	23,2%	100,0%
	1	Count	7	25	30	20	82
		% within Others – Students	8,5%	30,5%	36,6%	24,4%	100,0%
Total		Count	27	53	55	42	177
		% within Others – Students	15,3%	29,9%	31,1%	23,7%	100,0%

Table 7 shows the variables "Students"/ "Others" and their probability to continue the practise of football in more than five years. The 28% of students consider it to be "very probable", so there is a little increase, but there is a huge 23,2% of students who think the probability to continue football in more then five years, "not probable at all". Also here, the χ^2 test shows that there is not a significant relationship between the variables $[\chi^2= 5,396; p= 0,145]$

Table 7: *Relationship between the variables "Students-Others" and "probability to continue football in more than five years"*

| | | | prob. to continue football in more than five years | | | | |
			not probable at all	2	3	very probable	Total
Others (0) – Students (1)	0	Count	36	29	13	17	95
		% within Others – Students	37,9%	30,5%	13,7%	17,9%	100,0%
	1	Count	19	29	11	23	82
		% within Others – Students	23,2%	35,4%	13,4%	28,0%	100,0%
Total		Count	55	58	24	40	177
		% within Others – Students	31,1%	32,8%	13,6%	22,6%	100,0%

As it was predictable, there is a decrease of probability for the long-term decisions. So there are more students thinking probable playing football in the next three years, than in more than five years. As the mean average of the age of the respondents is 21 years old, these results perfectly reflect the uncertainty that is typical of that age and of the students.

Although the results confirm the reality, the χ^2 of all the three cross tabulation, shown by *Table 5, Table 6, Table 7*, are not significant. It means that there is not a significant relationship between the variables.

Chapter 7

Interview to Mr. Roberto Genta

One aim of my thesis is to investigate what could be done for the women's football development. So I created a question in my questionnaire where I ask to the athletes their point of view and what can be the relevant factors that can help the improvement of women's football. The findings show that 82,7% of the interviewees think the factor "more media attention" as very important and able grow the level of development of this specific sport. It is followed by the factor "more sponsors" that is thought to be from the 77,8% of people as very important. Than comes the factor "falling of socio-cultural barriers that see women's football only as a male game" with a 66,5% of girls considering it to be very important. Interesting to notice is that the factor that received the lowest score of consensus is "more prepared coach" that has been scored from the 5,9% of the respondents with not important at all and 24,3% with not important.

Than I concentrated on the FIFA Women World Cup 2011. I found interesting to ask what they really think that FIFA WWC can bring to women's football, giving some relevant factors that has been scored on a Likert-scale from 1, not important at all, to 4, very important. The results show that athletes think that the FIFA WWC will bring exactly what they thought to be necessary for the women's football development. So actually there is a sort of high optimisms and high reliability of the big event. As a matter of fact, the factor that obtained the highest consensus from the respondents is "more media attention" with a mean average of 2,98 followed by "more sponsors" with a mean average of 2,73.

After this analysis I wanted to look further into the perspectives and problematic of women's football, so I decided to contact my friend and ex-coach Mr. Roberto Genta to make an interview. Roberto Genta is 40 years old and works in the women's football world since he was 24. He began his activity as goalkeeper trainer and than he start to be the coach of some youth teams. After that he coached teams of the second division, first division and also premiere league. He worked in the marketing field and for some television and radio programs. He is now employed as journalist for the Website *calciodonne.it*

I met Roberto in Verona in April 2011 and I asked him 9 questions about the expectations, perception, problematic and the changes of women's football in Italy.

In the appendix I report the interview, naturally hold in Italian, as Roberto is Italian.

This interview helped me to have another important point of view that comes from the internal world of women's football. I asked Roberto some questions regarding the significant changes that he noticed during the years and also what is actually not changed in the women's football world.

About this last topic, he said that some important changes have been made as for example the technical-tactical preparation of the teams with the entry of specialized trainers. Some improvements are visible in the organisation of the football societies, the staff is more prepared and the formative path of the athletes seems to be more professional. However, we have to state that the starting point of these improvements was so low that the general development is not sufficient to generate relevant increments. The reason why is because the women's football world is full of persons that love this game, but misses persons with the right managerial aptitude. A problem that seems to slow down the development of women's football is the homophobia. Like many other sports that need physical contact, it is usual to find homosexual girls. As consequence, frightened parents do not want to let their daughters play football because they think they could be influenced.

Thant the interview moves on the differences between male and women's football. The answer is very clear, football is football and for this reason there are no differences in this discipline whether masculine or feminine. There are rather differences in the general management of the societies and the teams. Persons responsible for the evolution of women's football are not able or even worst, not interested in making women's football a developed sport. This disinterest, thinks Mr. Genta, is the real problem of women's football.

To the question about what could the FIFA WWC bring to women's football, Mr. Genta answer that women's football, due to the lack of show, is not yet a product for such big event. Thus he considers the World Championship as a way to make this sport more popular.

Than I wanted to know if there are some relevant differences between us and the European countries always speaking about the women's football field. Roberto said that he does not know too much about the foreign women's football but he considers a strong political interest as important factor to make women's football begin his development. The schools should be places where to find this type of sport where all the girls could play this beautiful game. If this could be possible, the socio-cultural barriers that see football only as mal game and the fear of homosexuality would immediately fall. Moreover there will be more athletes, which actually could be considered one of the lacks of women's football to have such a little number of players. After that the football teams should all include a women's team in their organic as it already happens for some foreign countries. In this way they could have at least the sufficient monetary sustain to do not fall as usually happens in the women's football world. Finally the female premiere league must become professional.

The last question I asked Mr. Genta is "Do you think that in the future, women's football could be similar to USA women's football?". He thinks that in this current world where we live, everything could happen. Thanks to the media, in one day you can become a star. So it could also happens for women's football but before it some important changes have to be made.

Chapter 8

Discussions and conclusions

A really interesting fact that emerged from the analysis of the results relates to the interaction between the factors "find new friends" and "socialize with my friends" in the motivation to practise women's football. It is important to remember that "find new friends" is found in the question about the initial factors that push women toward the practise of football, while "socialize with my friends" is related to the question about the current factors. Generally you are lead to think that "find new friends" can be one of the most important factor pushing anyone toward the beginning of a sport activity. Actually on the basis of my investigations, this factor seems to be not relevant in the choice to start practising football for girls. While it appears to be more relevant to continue the practise of this sport. Actually it is interesting to read what Bouet (1966) writes after the conduction of an investigation about the social aspect of sport: "Investigations carried out by us concerning the motives for the practise of sport have shown that many people look through sport for contacts with other humans. Many persons among those investigated say that while at first they were not interested in the acquisition of colleagues, yet later, after having chosen a concrete sport field; they began to be directly interested in it. They maintain their ties with those colleagues even when they no longer practise sport actively [...]. What, however, would be left of sport if it were deprived of that characteristic of community and friendship?"

So the author wants to say that there is more the willingness to maintain friends in the sport environment rather than the willingness to make new friends while approaching a new sport environment. If we make a little comparison between the mean average of the factor "find new friends" related to the question about the elements initially influencing the practise of football and "socialize with my friends" that is part of the question about the current elements influencing the practise of football, we can see that "find new friends" obtained s mean average of 2,02 while "socialize with my friends" 2,91. If we look further, as reported in the analysis of the results, 29% of the interviewees consider the factor "socialize with my friends" to be very important and only 9% consider "find new friends" as an important factor to start playing football. Actually these results confirm what Bouet (1966) wrote about this argument.

Another aspect that I want to take into consideration regards the factor "share a common identity". It is part of the question about the current factors pushing women toward the practise of football. This factor obtained only 2,31 of mean average and in my opinion it is quite low result if we consider that it wants to evidence the demand of being a woman playing a typical male game. Women's football, as all the other minor sports, is not too much developed and it is unusual to hear about it. For this reason being a player of that determinate minor sport, let you be part of something that is unique and that is reserved only for few persons. So it is interesting to notice that in the literature review, minor sport's events have said to play a strong importance and can become a way to express the sense of belonging to that sport.

Green (2001) wrote an article about women flag football players and in particular about a huge tournament that takes place in the Key West, Florida. She writes "Opportunities for participants to parade and celebrate their identities, as women footballers are vital. In particular, opportunities to share informally with other women who also identify with the subculture are important".

During my analysis I found also interesting to go into more depth about the factors representing the educational aspects of motivation.

I inserted to different aspects that could but be associated, one concerning the initial push "my teachers at school" and the other concerning the current push, "the coach pushes me". In both cases they received the lowest score of mean average. So we can state that athletes think that coaches and teachers do not have any relevant importance that could motivate themselves toward the practise of football.

Surprising to notice are the results obtained by asking the question "What do you think can help women's football becoming a more popular and developed sport? ". The factor "more prepared coach " received also here the lowest score of mean average (2,99). So actually women's football players give no importance to preparation of the coaches. Form the results emerge that there is a general lack of confidence for the educative figures, make the athletes thinking that coaches and teachers cannot have any type of influence on motivation and on an improvement of this sport.

In my opinion, these results reflect a particular situation where real professional figures like coaches and trainers are missing to women's football. These persons should motivate and push their athletes toward the practise of sport. For what concerning teachers, as also Mr. Genta said during his interview, the women's football revolution should start from the basis and more in specific teachers at school should motivate and let kids trying different sports. Very important is that there must be the possibility for every child to approach to different type of sports especially those that are not gender-related, in order to let these anachronistic socio-cultural barriers fall.

Dealing with motivation toward the practise of women's football, I can make some important conclusions about the initial and than current factors pushing girls. The factors that received the highest mean average score about the initial push are, "I used to watch football matches on TV" (2,8), "sport is important for the maintenance and development of a healthy body" (2,58) and "there was a team in the neighbourhood"(2,25). So, on the basis of my results, ladies are initially pushed by the desire to emulate football idols and by the convenience of having a women's football team in the neighbourhood. On the basis of SDT, Self Determinant Theory, discovered and developed by Deci and Ryan (1985), I can conclude that female football players are *extrinsic motivated* toward the practise of football because of the high rate of the factor "sport is important for the maintenance and development of a healthy body" that is connected with *Identification*, a specific type of Extrinsic Motivation, also found in the Deci and Ryan (1985) research.

Identified motivations relate to athletes that decide to do sport because they feel that in this way they can grow and develop as a person. These individuals value and judge actions as important and necessary for they own growth and they perform it out of choice.

Concerning the motivation currently pushing women toward the practise of football, the factors that obtained the highest mean average score are, "passion" (3,72), "the pleasure felt playing" (3,67) and "the pleasure felt during matches" (3,5). So, I can conclude saying that ladies are currently pushed by passion toward the practise of football. This factor could not easily be explained, measured and they vary across different persons. Moreover they are *intrinsic motivated*, in specific, to experience stimulation, because of the high mean average rate of "pleasure felt playing" and "pleasure felt during matches". However there is an influence of both *task and ego orientation*. Because of the first factor, we can state that athletes have the tendency to improve themselves without looking at the other, so signal of *task orientation*, while for the second factor, there is an influence of *ego orientation* due to the willingness to the competition against the opponent.

Task orientation and *Ego orientation* are the two motivational tendencies found in AGT, Achievement Goal Theory, developed by Hagger and Chatzisarantis (2005).

Task orientation refers to an athlete that does sports in order to learn new skills, improve himself without looking at the others. In the *Ego orientation* the athlete is looking for competition against the opponent and the most important thing is to show the predominance.

Often *Task orientation* (AGT) is connected with *Intrinsic Motivation* (SDT) because the assumptions of Task orientation could be signals of an internal motivation.

During my thesis I classified women's football as minor sport for many motivations. For this reasons I wanted to delineate a general profile showing how athletes see their sport, their level of information about it and the possible solutions that could be adopted to help the development of women's football.

About this last aspect the results obtained show that the two most important factors that can help women's football to become a more developed and popular game are "more media attention" with 3,79 mean average and "more sponsors" with 3,68. So, as also underlined in the Literature review, these are the two main factors that permit generation of money and flow of news and information, two important ingredients to transform a minor sport into a more followed and considered sport.

As usual since 1991, every four years the FIFA Women World Cup takes place. This current year, 2011, it took place in Germany. I asked my interviewees if they knew about this important event. From the results I found that 77% of the respondents knew about it, while 23% did not know anything. This 77% could initially appear as a good percentage, however if we think about the size and impact of such an event, this unaware 23% results to be a too much big number. Naturally the reason for this low attention to the sport at international level can be connect with the disinterest of the athletes but also with the low media attention that do not permit the right flow of news.

About the FIFA WWC I found interesting to ask my interviewees what they aspect it will bring to women's football. The most scored factors were "more media attention" with 2,98 mean average and "more sponsors" with 2,73. As we can clearly see they are exactly the factors needed for the development of women's football. So I can conclude saying that athletes are very optimistic towards the benefits brought FIFA WWC.

The last analysis I conducted consisted in examining some variables in order to understand if there is a significant relationship between them. I reached my aim using SPSS and conducting the statistical methods called χ^2 tests. It permits me to observe the significance "p" that must be [p< 0,05] in order to have the two variables being dependent each other.

I decided to put into relationship the variables awareness "Did you know about the FIFA WWC?" and the statements about which factors are needed to improve women's football. I created a cross tabulation for every single statement in relation to the question about the FIFA WWC. From the results obtained, there are only two χ^2 tests that are significant. These are obtained by the relationship between the awareness of FIFA WWC and the factor "more competent managers" [χ^2=14,827 and p= 0,002], and the awareness of FIFA WWC and the factor "more suitable structures" [χ^2= 9,244; p= 0,026]. The other tests are not significant, so there is no relationship between the variables.

The other variables I put into relationship were "initial push of the teachers" and "more prepared coaches", "current push of coaches" and "more prepared coaches",

"Students"/ "Others" and the probability to continue the practise of football in the next three years, "Students"/ "Others" and the probability to continue the practise of football in the next five years, "Students"/ "Others" and the probability to continue the practise of football in more than five years. Unfortunately all the χ^2 tests for these variables result to be not significant.

This research work presents some limitations mainly due to sampling techniques. Concerning the collection of the data, there was no control due to the fact that the questionnaires were put online, on social networks and distributed also with the snowball sampling technique. Another constraint that I had to face was related to the fact that many of the respondents were Italians. Although I tried to reach as much persons from all over the world as I could, I found it hard. I spread around my questionnaire trying to focus on international women's football web pages and social networks. Despite all my effort, I could only collect 8 questionnaires from people outside Italy. Moreover, due to monetary and budget constraints, I collected in total only 185 questionnaires. On one side, this number of questionnaires allows me to make some analysis, but on the other side it appears to be insufficient. As I do not know how many girls are currently playing football in Italy, I should have collected a minimum of 400 questionnaires for my research to be representative. So, the main limitation of this research is that the sample is not fully representative.

8.1 FUTURE RESEARCH

This research work could actually be developed using a bigger sample. With time and monetary possibilities 400 questionnaires should be easily collected in order to make the sample representative. Moreover the collection of data would be more precise. More interviews could be done and the questionnaires could be made face to face. Also more international people could be reached in order to have a more specific overview about the situation out of Italy.

Nevertheless this research gives a first overview about the challenges of minor sports such as women's football and provides the basis to further explore the motivations that push women toward the practise of football.

References

Bouet, M. (1966). The Function of Sport in Human Relations. *International Review for the Sociology of Sport*, 1 (1), pp. 137-140.

Cratty, B. (1974). *Psychologie et activitè phisique*. Paris, Vigot Frères.

Cumminga S. P.; Smithb R. E.; Smollb F. L.; Standagea M.; Grossbard J. R. (2008) Development and validation of the Achievement Goal Scale for Youth Sports. *Psychology of Sport and Exercise, 9*, pp.686–703.

Davis, N. (December 22nd, 2010). Can Women's soccer survive in America?. Games people play. http://www.theawl.com/2010/12/can-womens-soccer-survive-in-america. Accessed 10 th of April 2011, at 12:56.

De Beni, R. and Moè, A. (2000). *Motivazione e apprendimento*. Bologna, Il Mulino.

Deci, E.L. (1975). *Intrinsic Motivation*. New York, Plenum Press.

Deci, E.L. & Ryan, R.M. (1985). *Intrinsic Motivation and self-determination in human behavior*. New York, Plenum Press.

Deci, E.L. & Ryan, R.M. (2000). Self-Determination Theory and the Facilitation of Intrinsic Motivation, Social Development, and Well-Being. *American Psychologist*, 55 (1), pp. 68-78.

Duda, J. L. (1989). Relationship between task and ego orientation and the perceived purpose of sport among high school athletes. *Journal of Sport & Exercise Psychology*, 11, pp. 318–335.

Dweck, C. & Leggett, E. (1988). A social-cognitive approach to motivation and personality. *Psychological Review, 95*, pp. 256–273.

Elliot, A. (1997). *Integrating the "classic" and "contemporary" approaches to achievement motivation: A hierarchical model of approach and avoidance achievement motivation*. In M. Maehr, & P. Pintrich (Eds.), Advances in motivation and achievement, 10, pp. 143–179. Greenwich, CT: JAI Press.

Fortier M. S.; Vallerand R. J.; Brière N. M.; Provencher P. J. (1995). Competitive and Recreational Sport Structures and Gender: a test of their relationship with Sport Motivation. *International Journal Sport Psychology*; 26, pp. 26, 24-39.

Garry, W. (2000) *Sport and the media. Handbook of sports studies.* Sage Publications.

Gillet N.; Vallerand R. J.; Amoura S.; Baldes B. (2010). Influence of coaches' autonomy support on athletes' motivation and sport performance: A test of the hierarchical model of intrinsic and extrinsic motivation. *Psychology of Sport and Exercise 11*, pp. 155 and 161.

Green, C. B. (2001). Leveraging subculture and identity to promote sport events. *Sport Management Review.*

Greenhalgh G. P.; Simmons J. M., Hambrick M. E.; Greenwell T. C. (2011). Spectator Support: Examining the Attributes That Differentiate Niche from Mainstream Sport. *Sport Marketing Quarterly*, pp. 20, 41-52.

Hagger, M. and Chatzisarantis, N. (2005). *The Social Psychology of exercise and sport. Applying social psychology.* Series editor: Stephen Sutton.

Hagger, M.S. and Chatzisarantis N. (2007). *Intrinsic Motivation and Self-Determination in Exercise and Sport.* Human Kinetics Editions.

Howard L. and Nixon II (2008). *Sport in a changing world.* Pradigm Publisher, USA.

Kane, M.J & Parks J.B. (1992). *The social construction of gender difference and Hierarchy in sport jurnalism.* Stransford University Press.

Keegan R. J.; Harwood C. G.; Spray C. M.; Lavallee D. E. (2009). A qualitative investigation exploring the motivational climate in early career sports participants: Coach, parent and peer influences on sport motivation. *Psychology of Sport and Exercise 10*, pp. 361–372.

Maehr, M. L. and Zusho, A. (2009). Achievement Goal Theory, the past, present, and future. Handbook of motivation at school. Edited by Kathryn R. Wentzel and Allan Wigfield.

Malletta C.; Kawabataa M.; Newcombe P. (2007). Progressing measurement in sport motivation with the SMS-6: A response to Pelletier, Vallerand, and Sarrazin, *Psychology of Sport and Exercise*, pp. 622–631.

Malletta C.; Kawabataa M.; Newcombe P., Otero-Foreroa A.; Jacksona S. (2007). Sport motivation scale-6 (SMS-6): A revised six-factor sport motivation scale. *Psychology of Sport and Exercise*. pp. 600–614.

Messner, M. A. (2005). *Center of Attention: The gender of sports media. Sport and contemporary society: an anthology*. USA, Paradigm Publisher.

Messner, M. A.; Dunbar, M. and Hunt, D. (2000). The televised sports manhood formula. *Journal of sport and social issues*.

Nicholls, J. (1984). Achievement motivation: Conceptions of ability, subjective experience, task choice, and performance. *Psychological Review*, 91, pp. 328–346.

Nicholson, M. (2007*). Sport and the media, managing the nexus*. USA, Elsevier.

Pelletier L. G.; Tuson; Brière N. M; Fortier M. S; Vallerand R. J. (1995). Toward a New Measure of Intrinsic Motivation, Extrinsic Motivation, and Amotivation in Sports: The Sport Motivation Scale (SMS). *Journal of Sport & exercise psychology*. pp. 35-53.

Pelletier L. G.; Vallerand R. J.; Sarrazin P. (2007). The revised six-factor Sport Motivation Scale (Mallett, Kawabata, Newcombe, Otero-Forero, & Jackson, 2007): Something old, something new, and something borrowed. *Psychology of Sport and Exercise*. pp. 615–621.

Pintrich P. R; Conley A. M.; Kempler T. M (2003). Current issues in achievement goal theory and research. *International Journal of Educational Research, 39*, pp. 319–337.

Rosner, S. R. & Shropshire, K. L. (2004). Start-up leagues and niche sports. *The business of sports*, Sudbury, MA, Jones & Bartlett Publishers.

Ryan, R. M. (1995). Psychological needs and the facilitation of integrative processes. *Journal of Personality, 63*, pp. 397–427.

Sassatelli, R. (2003). *Sport e Genere. Lo sport al femminile*. Italia, Enciclopedia dello Sport Treccani.

Scardicchio, A. (2011). *Storia e storie di calcio femminile*. Calcio in rosa. Milano, Lampi di stampa.

Simonelli, G. and Ferrarotti, A. (1995). *I media nel pallone*. Milano, Guerini e Associati.

Sit, C. H. P. and Lindner, K. J. (2005). Motivational orientations in youth sport participation: Using Achievement Goal Theory and Reversal Theory. *Personality and Individual Differences 38*, pp. 605–618.

Trombino, M. (1998). *Giocare un gioco difficile*.Bari, La Terza.

Vallerand, R. J. (1997). *Toward a hierarchical model of intrinsic and extrinsic motivation*. In M. Zanna (Ed.), Advances in experimental social psychology (pp. 271–360). New York, Academic Press.

Vallerand R. J.; Brière N. M; Blais & Pelletier L. G. (in press). Development and validation of a measure of instrinsic, extrinsic and amotivation in sports: the Sport Motivation Scale (SMS). *Journal International de Psycholgie du Sport*.

Vanek, M. and Cratty, B. (1972) *Psychologie sportive et competition*. Paris, Universitaires.

Vansteenkiste, M. (2005). Intrinsic versus extrinsic goal framing and autonomy-support versus control: Promoting performance, persistence, well-being and socially adaptive functioning. *Unpublished doctoral dissertation*. University of Leuven, Belgium.

Vansteenkiste M.; Matos L.; Lens W.; Soenens B. (2007). Understanding the impact of intrinsic versus extrinsic goal framing on exercise performance: The conflicting role of task and ego involvement. *Psychology of Sport and Exercise 8*, pp. 771–794.

Williams, J. (2007). *A Beautiful Game. International perspectives on Women's football*. New York, Berg.

WEB SITES:

http://www.calciodonne.net

www.womensoccer.com

www.calcioinrosa.it

www.fifa.com

www.thefword.org.uk

www.theawl.com

Appendix

Interview to Mr. Roberto Genta

- *Da quanti anni lavora nel calcio femminile e che ruoli ha svolto o svolge all' interno di questo mondo?*

Lavoro nel calcio femminile da 24 anni, inizialmente come preparatore dei portieri visto il mio passato calcistico, successivamente ho allenato settori giovanili per poi passare alle prime squadre. Serie C, serie B, serie A2 e per finire serie A. Mi sono sempre occupato di marketing e di visibilità lavorando intensamente con testate televisive e radiofoniche.

- *Ha visto cambiamenti significativi da quando ha iniziato la sua attività nel calcio femminile?*

Sicuramente ci sono stati cambiamenti importanti nel mondo del calcio femminile, ma ciò che è stato fatto è veramente poco. Le singole persone lavorano intensamente, ma per garantire continuità a questo sport serve un collettivo forte e non la singola iniziativa sporadica.

- *Se si quali sono i cambiamenti?*

Credo che molti cambiamenti siano stati fatti per quanto concerne la parte relativa alla preparazione tecnico-tattica delle formazioni e con l'ingresso di preparatori atletici specializzati, anche la parte atletica è migliorata molto in questi ultimi anni. Il fisico delle atlete è nettamente migliore rispetto al passato e anche l'organizzazione societaria ha subìto dei leggeri miglioramenti. Lo staff tecnico di molte società è visibilmente cresciuto e i percorsi formativi già dai settori giovanili hanno un' impronta nettamente più professionale. Purtroppo il punto di partenza era talmente basso che questi miglioramenti non risultano sufficienti per una crescita del movimento.

- *Se ritiene che non ci sia stato cambiamento, perchè?*

Qualche cambiamento c'e' stato, ma esso risulta insufficiente rispetto a ciò che servirebbe fare per rendere credibile questo movimento. Il perche non è stato fatto è molto semplice, mancano nel calcio femminile le persone che hanno uno spirito imprenditoriale e gestionale, mentre pullulano gli amatori del pallone e i risultati, purtroppo, sono alla luce del sole. A rallentare la crescita del calcio femminile di sicuro possiamo mettere l'omofobia. Come in tanti altri tipi di sport che richiedono contatto fisico, femminili e non, ma forse in particolar modo per il calcio femminile, non è strano trovare ragazze omosessuali. Di conseguenza si trovano genitori impauriti che bloccano l'approccio a questa disciplina per paura che la propria figlia si faccia influenzare.

- *Come vede il calcio femminile nei confronti del calcio maschile?*

Non vedo differenza alcuna, il calcio è calcio, ma come detto precedentemente la differenza viene fatta da chi governa il mondo del calcio femminile, dai dirigenti nazionali e regionali e da quelli delle singole realtà, che spesso risultano non adatti o poco interessati al miglioramento di questo movimento.

- *Quali sono attualmente le debolezze maggiori che affliggono il calcio femminile?*

L'incapacità manageriale della gestione del prodotto calcio femminile sia a livello nazionale che a livello locale.

- *Cosa si aspetta dai mondiali di calcio 2011 in Germania?*

Non ho grandi aspettative, il calcio femminile non è ancora un prodotto da grandi eventi per la mancanza di spettacolarità, ma credo che eventi di questo genere servano all'opinione pubblica per iniziare a conoscere questo bellissimo sport.

- *Vede differenze tra la realtà italiana e di altre nazioni?*

Conosco pochissimo delle realtà estere, ma credo che per far decollare il calcio femminile serva una volontà politica molto forte. Le scuole sono sicuramente il primo elemento dove potremmo risolvere da subito il problema relativo alla mancanza di atlete che scelgono questo sport. Secondariamente, credo che si potrebbero obbligare le formazioni maschili ad avere una formazione femminile così da iniziare ad avere alle spalle delle strutture societarie importanti in grado di dare continuità evitando il pessimo spettacolo dello scioglimento societario che ogni anno disfa numerose squadre di calcio femminile. Ho sentito che esperienze di questo genere sono state attuate in alcuni stati esteri con risultati importanti. Credo poi che almeno la serie A femminile debba essere inserita nello sport professionistico.

- *Secondo Lei il calcio femminile può arrivare ad avere un seguito simile a quello statunitense, si no, come?*

Nel mondo mediatico nel quale viviamo tutto può accadere. Esistono sconosciute che diventano star mondiali dopo essere andate ad una cena, quindi anche il calcio femminile può diventare uno sport molto seguito, ma come precedentemente detto, servono menti in grado creare interesse.

Crosstab

			more competent managers				
			Not important at all	2	3	Very important	Total
Do you know about the FIFA WWC ?	yes	Count	4	24	36	78	142
		% within do you know about FIFA WWC?	2.8%	16.9%	25.4%	54.9%	100.0%
	no	Count	4	5	21	12	42
		% within do you know about FIFA WWC?	9.5%	11.9%	50.0%	28.6%	100.0%
Total		Count	8	29	57	90	184
		% within do you know about FIFA WWC?	4.3%	15.8%	31.0%	48.9%	100.0%

Chi-Square Tests

	Value	df	Asymp. Sig. (2-sided)
Pearson Chi-Square	14.827[a]	3	.002
Likelihood Ratio	14.219	3	.003
Linear-by-Linear Association	5.124	1	.024
N of Valid Cases	184		

a. 1 cells (12,5%) have expected count less than 5. The minimum expected count is 1,83.

Crosstab

			more suitable structures				
			not important at all	2	3	very important	Total
Do you know about FIFA WWC?	yes	Count	6	23	58	54	141
		% within do you know about the FIFA WWC?	4.3%	16.3%	41.1%	38.3%	100.0%
	no	Count	3	15	10	14	42
		% within do you know about the FIFA WWC?	7.1%	35.7%	23.8%	33.3%	100.0%
Total		Count	9	38	68	68	183
		% within do you know about the FIFA WWC?	4.9%	20.8%	37.2%	37.2%	100.0%

Chi-Square Tests

	Value	df	Asymp. Sig. (2-sided)
Pearson Chi-Square	9.244[a]	3	.026
Likelihood Ratio	8.779	3	.032
Linear-by-Linear Association	3.789	1	.052
N of Valid Cases	183		

a. 1 cells (12,5%) have expected count less than 5. The minimum expected count is 2,07.

| | | | more prapared coaches | | | | |
			not important at all	2	3	very important	Total
current push from coaches	not important at all	Count	6	16	18	30	70
		% within current push form coaches	8,6%	22,9%	25,7%	42,9%	100,0%
	2	Count	3	20	19	23	65
		% within current push form coaches	4,6%	30,8%	29,2%	35,4%	100,0%
	3	Count	1	7	19	7	34
		% within current push form coaches	2,9%	20,6%	55,9%	20,6%	100,0%
	very important	Count	1	2	5	6	14
		% within current push form coaches	7,1%	14,3%	35,7%	42,9%	100,0%
Total		Count	11	45	61	66	183
		% within current push form coaches	6,0%	24,6%	33,3%	36,1%	100,0%

Chi-square tests

	Value	df	Asymp. Sig. (2-sided)
Pearson Chi-Square	13,556[a]	9	,139
Likelihood Ratio	13,246	9	,152
Linear-by-Linear Association	,000	1	,997
N of Valid Cases	183		

a. 6 celle (37,5%) hanno un conteggio atteso inferiore a 5. Il conteggio atteso minimo è ,84.

| | | | more prepared coaches | | | | |
			not important at all	2	3	very important	Total
initial push of the teachers	not important at all	Count	10	41	55	52	158
		% within initial push from teachers	6,3%	25,9%	34,8%	32,9%	100,0%
	2	Count	0	1	5	9	15
		% within initial push from teachers	,0%	6,7%	33,3%	60,0%	100,0%
	3	Count	1	3	0	2	6
		% within initial push from teachers	16,7%	50,0%	,0%	33,3%	100,0%
	very important	Count	0	0	2	3	5
		% within initial push from teachers	,0%	,0%	40,0%	60,0%	100,0%
Total		Count	11	45	62	66	184
		% within initial push from teachers	6,0%	24,5%	33,7%	35,9%	100,0%

Chi-square tests

	Value	df	Asymp. Sig. (2-sided)
Pearson Chi-Square	13,066[a]	9	,160
Likelihood Ratio	17,000	9	,049
Linear-by-Linear Association	2,000	1	,157
N of Valid Cases	184		

a. 10 celle (62,5%) hanno un conteggio atteso inferiore a 5. Il conteggio atteso minimo è ,30.

		prob. to continue football in the next 3 years				
			not probable at all	2	3	very probable	Total
Others (0) – Students (1)	0	Count	7	18	21	49	95
		% within Others – Students	7,4%	18,9%	22,1%	51,6%	100,0%
	1	Count	5	7	30	40	82
		% within Others – Students	6,1%	8,5%	36,6%	48,8%	100,0%
Total		Count	12	25	51	89	177
		% within Others – Students	6,8%	14,1%	28,8%	50,3%	100,0%

Chi–square tests

	Value	df	Asymp. Sig. (2–sided)
Pearson Chi–Square	6,753ᵃ	3	,080
Likelihood Ratio	6,897	3	,075
Linear–by–Linear Association	,522	1	,470
N of Valid Cases	177		

a. 0 celle (,0%) hanno un conteggio atteso inferiore a 5. Il conteggio atteso minimo è 5,56.

		prob. to continue football in more than five years				
			not probable at all	2	3	very probable	Total
Others (0) – Students (1)	0	Count	36	29	13	17	95
		% within Others – Students	37,9%	30,5%	13,7%	17,9%	100,0%
	1	Count	19	29	11	23	82
		% within Others – Students	23,2%	35,4%	13,4%	28,0%	100,0%
Total		Count	55	58	24	40	177
		% within Others – Students	31,1%	32,8%	13,6%	22,6%	100,0%

Chi–square tests

	Value	df	Asymp. Sig. (2–sided)
Pearson Chi–Square	5,396ᵃ	3	,145
Likelihood Ratio	5,456	3	,141
Linear–by–Linear Association	4,152	1	,042
N of Valid Cases	177		

a. 0 celle (,0%) hanno un conteggio atteso inferiore a 5. Il conteggio atteso minimo è 11,12.

			prob. to continue football in the next five years				
			not probable at all	2	3	very probable	Total
Others (0) – Students (1)	0	Count	20	28	25	22	95
		% within Others – Students	21,1%	29,5%	26,3%	23,2%	100,0%
	1	Count	7	25	30	20	82
		% within Others – Students	8,5%	30,5%	36,6%	24,4%	100,0%
Total		Count	27	53	55	42	177
		% within Others – Students	15,3%	29,9%	31,1%	23,7%	100,0%

Chi-square tests

	Value	df	Sig. asint. (2 vie)
Pearson Chi-Square	6,057[a]	3	,109
Likelihood Ratio	6,291	3	,098
Associazione lineare-lineare	2,757	1	,097
N. di casi validi	177		

a. 0 celle (,0%) hanno un conteggio atteso inferiore a 5. Il conteggio atteso minimo è 12,51.